Jack McClelland: The Pride of Pittsburg

By Vincent T. Ciaramella

Win By KO Publications
Iowa City

Jack McClelland: The Pride of Pittsburg

Vincent T. Ciaramella

(ISBN-13): 978-0-9903703-9-0

(hardcover: 50# acid-free alkaline paper)

Includes bibliography.

© 2018 by Vincent T. Ciaramella. All Rights Reserved.

No part of this book may be reproduced, or transmitted in any form or by any means, graphic, electronic or mechanical, including photocopying, recording, taping, or by any information storage retrieval system without the written permission of Vincent T. Ciaramella.

Cover design by Gwyn Snider ©

Manufactured in the United States of America.

Win By KO Publications
Iowa City, Iowa
winbykopublications.com

Dedication

To my awesome son and best friend, Enzo. Dream it and create it. I love you!

In loving memory of my grandfather, Thomas Hardinger.

Acknowledgements

This book would not be possible without the love and support of many people.

First, I would like to thank Douglas Cavanaugh, Claudia Ciaramella, Shirley & Nick Quaquarucci, and Lisa McClelland for their help in researching Jack. Without you five, this book would have never come into existence.

Second, I would also like to thank my loving wife, Erika and my mom, Mariann Mellinger for suggesting the idea that I write this book.

Third, I would like to thank my friends and family, especially Reverend Dennis O'Leary Jr., for their support and encouragement along the way.

Fouth, I would like to thank Jen Sequel for working with the photos in the book and for bringing them back to life.

Fifth, I would like to thank National Police Gazette Enterprises, LLC for the usage of the image on the front cover.

Sixth, I would like to thank John Schalcosky, founder of The Odd, Mysterious & Facincating History of Pittsburgh for helping me learn to use the mapping programs which uncovered the current locations of the fight sites.

Lastly, I would like to thank my son, Enzo for riding along with me on this journey all over Pittsburgh while I researched this book. You rock, good sir!

Preface

There is just something about sports from the late nineteenth and early twentieth century that fascinates me. From Pedestrianism to feats of strength performed by Louis Cyr to Captain Matthew Webb's epic swim across the English Channel, this era of athletics has always held a vice like grip on my imagination. While all of the aforementioned persons and sports are enthralling, boxing and the boxers of this period are the undisputed champions of my mind.

First, I should mention that I am the great-great grandson of Jack *The Pride of Pittsburg* McClelland. Maybe that is why boxing has always had such an appeal for me. I grew up playing Punch Out on Nintendo, watching Mike Tyson box, and wishing I knew more about this person in my family. This was the 1980's and the internet was not part of everyday life. What I knew about the man at that time was that he was a boxer that fought on barges on the river, and his son, John, was my great-grandfather. That is it.

My family did not talk about him because he left my great-great grandmother, Rose. The older generation back then did not like to dredge up the past. So, for the first thirty-seven years of my life that is all I knew about him. Fast forward to 2015.

One night I was surfing the internet, just looking up nothing to pass the time. Jack popped into my head and for the first time I decided to look him up. What I found was an Ebay listing for newspaper clippings and copies of pictures. I couldn't believe my luck! I used the "buy-it-now" option and twelve dollars later I had more info than I thought I would ever have. After the package arrived with all my new information, I spent a few hours just reading, putting the information in order, and trying to put everything into context. When I was done, I knew there were large holes missing in both his personal and professional life. But where else to turn? As luck would have it, I began a correspondence with Douglas Cavanaugh of *Pittsburgh Boxing: A Pictorial History* on Facebook. He had information and photos that I did not. So we traded and I was able to fill in more.

Then, my Aunt Claudia got involved and she knew more about him than I could find on the internet. It was all coming together. However, what really sealed the deal was a chance meeting on a cool fall Thursday afternoon in November 2017.

After looking for weeks for information about his final resting place, I finally hit pay dirt. The Highwood Cemetery staff was kind enough to send me the info containing his plot information as well as a copy of an index card that listed his cause of death and his last known address. How could I be so lucky! So off I went to photograph both his grave and his last residence. When I got to the home, it looked deserted. I went up onto the porch and the mailbox was overflowing with junk mail. None of the mail had the same name. I concluded this must be a rental property. I looked in the window and there was no furniture or signs of anyone living there. I was bummed. I was hoping that the people there might have some information but it looked like I was about to strike out. Walking back to my car I looked at the house next door and saw the nice manicured lawn and Steeler flags. I thought, "Go knock, what can it hurt?"

As I walked up the stairs towards the front door, I prayed that I wouldn't see a double barrel sticking in my face or a large dog that might use me as a chew toy. I saw a woman at a table in the window and she looked friendly enough, I was just hoping she felt the same about me. Her husband, Nick answered the door. I introduced myself and asked if he knew the people next door. He said that nobody had lived there in over a decade. I decided to go for broke and I told him that I was doing some research about my great-great grandfather who was a boxer and gave him Jack's name. By this time, Shirley was at the door and her eyes got big. Nick said, "She is a McClelland." I could not believe it. I asked if she knew Jack McClelland and she replied that he was her grandfather. I then held out my hand and said, "I am Jack's great-great grandson." What luck! They invited me in, along with my wife, Erika, and son Enzo, who is Jack's great-great-great grandson. We sat at their kitchen table and within minutes, she produced a collection the likes I had never seen before of articles and photographs, along with his cabinet cards. I hit the motherlode. She was even kind enough to allow me to take all of it to copy as long as I brought it back. I told her I would be back on Saturday and that I wanted to interview her. She agreed and just like that, I had almost all my information. Call it fate, divine intervention, or just random chance, either way I was beyond the moon happy. I returned that Saturday and I did my interview. A few weeks later, after doing more research via the web through newspapers.com I had all the information that I needed. The book came together so quickly and simply that it felt like it was meant to be.

What you hold in your hands is the first ever biography of Jack McClelland, an important figure in early boxing history. Jack was extremely influential in both Pittsburgh and across the country. At one time, he was one of the greatest featherweights in the division. Sadly, his fame and story were lost to time for a variety of reasons and all but the diehard boxing historian still remembers his name. Armed with all my information I felt it was time to pluck him from obscurity and place him back among the greats of his era. I have written three works of fiction and two pieces of scholarship published on Homer and the play Agamemnon through the Center of Hellenistic Studies, a division of Harvard University, so I had no qualms about writing this book.

When reading this work know that, everything was checked and rechecked using multiple sources when available. Everything you read is rooted in historical fact and can be checked by anyone using the information in the bibliography. I kept as neutral a tone as I could throughout the book, as I did not want to show bias based on my family connection. Jack is presented here, warts and all. While this preface is written in an informal style, the pages that follow are crafted using the voice and tone of scholarship.

In closing, I hope you enjoy this journey through the late Victorian era of boxing history. It is my hope that this book not only entertains but enlightens as well. So ladies and gentleman. At the sound of the gong come out of your corners and start reading!

Vincent T. Ciaramella

04/07/2018

Introduction

The story of Jack McClelland is the story of a man climbing the mountain but falling to his death just before he reaches the top. There is a tragic quality and one that is completely relatable to anyone that gave it his or her best but fell short of the mark for whatever reason. Jack was a man rooted in the late Victorian era of Pittsburgh but his rise and fall is a timeless story that can be found in any age. Before the reader begins their journey though the life of Jack McClelland, the author wants to clear up some aspects of this book that might confuse the reader.

First, the missing "h" in Pittsburgh. Pittsburgh's "h" was dropped in 1891 to create a unified spelling of all cities that had "burg" in their name. Unlike the German "burg", the Pittsburgh "h" comes from Scotland. John Forbes, a Scottish officer during the French and Indian War most likely had a pronouncation close to Edinburgh in mind when he named the city, hence it should sound like Pitts-borough. It was not restored until July of 1911.

Throughout this book, you may see the "h" and then not see it the next time. The reason behind this is dependent on the context and time I am writing about or referencing. If it is post 1911 you will see an "h", if it is prior then there is no "h" as in "Pride of Pittsburg".

Second, newspapers during this period were unreliable and often did not fact check. This is why I tried to use as may sources as possible. I wanted to make sure that the reader was given the closest possible account of what happened. All of these multiple sources have led to an obese bibliography. What the reader might notice is the lack of footnote numbers in superscript. The reason for this is because so many sources were used that the text would become gridlocked and it would render the book esthetically unpleasing and distracting. If the reader is inclined, they can reconstruct the book by using the bibliography. Everything is in order from start to finish. Every quote and fact is there, sometimes in multiple sources.

Third, Turner Hall. Turner Halls were all over the Pittsburgh area during this time. Jack fought or attended events at multiple

Turner Halls. I tried to distinguish which location with its unique address. Therefore, the reader will see one in Manchester, one on Forbes, and others in different locations. However, not all have an address listed. If there is no unique address then there is not one given in any of the sources.

Finally, the use of the term "colored fighter". While this term would not be acceptable today, the phrase was common during the late nineteenth and early twentieth century. I use this term in the strictest of historical sense and mean no disrespect or offense to anyone. Being a stickler for historical accuracy, it must be included.

Now that you are armed with the information it should help you navigate the text without interruption or question. Enjoy the work and enjoy your journey back in time.

1873-1895

On February 2, 1895, a twenty-two year old fighter from the Hill District entered the Emerald Athletic Club and stepped into the ring for the first time. His name was Jack McClelland later known as *The Pride of Pittsburg*. Although his first bout yielded a loss in the third round to Tommy Mitchell, his switch from amateur to professional was just a year away. Jack would soon become one of the greatest fighters that Pittsburgh ever produced. During the Golden Age of Boxing, he was a minor celebrity in Western Pennsylvania, West Virginia, and Ohio and traveled as far west as Washington State for a fight, with plans to go to England that fell though. Jack McClelland's name and history would begin to fade from public memory by the Second World War. He became a forgotten figure in the early history of Pittsburgh boxing, only remembered by diehard fans and boxing historians.

It is now the year 2018, one hundred and twenty-three years since his first match. His children are all gone. He has one surviving grandchild. All his peers in the boxing world have passed. He lies buried in Highwood Cemetery off Brighton Road in Pittsburgh with no stone to mark his final resting place.

The author's intent is to bring Jack McClelland back from the dead for one last moment in the spotlight in hopes that he will inspire others to research these long forgotten sports heroes and maybe to inspire future pugilists who will look to him for inspiration.

Today, the Hill District in Pittsburgh, Pennsylvania is a lower income African-American neighborhood. PPG Paints Arena, the home of the five time Stanley Cup Champions, The Pittsburgh Penguins sits atop what was once low-income housing during the latter part of the 19th century through the middle of the 20th. The area attracted people from all different ethnic backgrounds including African-Americans, Italians, Russians, Syrians, Lebanese, and people of Irish/Scots-Irish descent who worked in the mills that filled the skies of Pittsburgh with smoke and ash. It was a rough part of town, and it still is today but its history is rich in jazz music, athletes, and the setting for some of August Wilson's plays, including his greatest work *"Fences"*. In an unassuming house that one would walk past without giving a second thought, a featherweight fighter was born.

John "Jack" McClelland was born on August 18, 1873 (though some sources mistakenly say 1874) to a poor Scots-Irish Protestant family. His older brother, William would one-day father Dr. William D. McClelland, five-time Allegheny County Coroner and chairman of the boxing commission. Jack did not set out to become a boxer. In fact, in an interview with the *Pittsburgh Sun-Telegraph* he states that he never really had any interest in the sport other than to make money. When asked would he box if he could do it all over again he replied "*no*" and that maybe he would have become a surveyor. This is very different from fighters today who crave the attention and fame that goes along with the sport.

There is scant information about Jack's early years. The quote below comes from an article published in the August 5, 1910 edition of the *Pittsburgh Press*:

"When but a youngster Mac shone as a postilion boy on the Wylle [sic] avenue horse car line. His duty was to ride down the extra pair of nags used to help the midget cars up the heavy grade from Tunnel Street to Fulton."

His father was a mill worker who on Saturdays partook in a brutal blood sport known as "*Mill Fights*". This was really just another name for back alley bare-knuckles boxing. Jack, who was devastating with his left, had this to say about his father:

"But the best left hand I ever saw was on my father. He used to work in the mill and they would have fights every Saturday afternoon just for the fun of it. The first man to draw blood was the winner, and the left hand of my old man's always poked'em in the nose and drew what they used to call claret."

After high school in the early 1890's, Jack began working with candy-maker and part-time boxer, Loudon Campbell, pulling taffy. Campbell was credited by Jack for getting him into boxing and teaching him how to hit with his left. Like many young and up-and-coming fighters, Jack favored his right. Campbell gave him a piece of advice that he would never forget about the left:

"That's the hand that wins fights."

Later in life, Jack would recall:

"It took me about two years of hard work to master the left, but once I had it down I had one of the best left hands in the business, a cutting jab and a hook which I used with a simple sight turn of the wrist. It was a left to the solar plexus that dropped Attell."

This is all we know about Jack's pre-fight life. According to his granddaughter, Shirley Quaquarucci, he never talked about his past and all she knew about his childhood was that he was born somewhere in the Hill District. Like many people of his generation, the past was the past and not something to dredge up.

Jack got his start boxing as an amateur in early 1895. His weight of 115 put him in the featherweight class on February 2 against Mitchell. Just six days later on February 8 at the Lyceum in McKeesport, Pennsylvania, he would weigh in at 125 when he took on Hugh Jones (also referenced as James) in the preliminaries of a tournament and defeated him. In the semifinals, he fought Jack Bennett (a future welterweight contender who would go on to fight three battles with lightweight champion Joe Gans), and won but withdrew from the contest in favor of Mike Tunny, who defeated Pat Malloy in the finals and won the medal on February 9.

February 22 and 23, Jack entered a tournament at the West End Gym. He weighed in this time at 115 when he took on Charles Schmepp, a first time fighter. During the fight, Schmepp took advantage of a rule that allowed fighters to tie their shoe or blow their nose without fear of being hit. He would rush at Jack, hit him with a straight right then left, back off, pretend to blow his nose, and look wickedly at McClelland from over his gloves. The fight lasted for three rounds with Jack winning. Schempp never boxed again. McClelland later took on Jack Kinlow in the finals. The people in attendance thought Mac stood no chance of winning but in the second round, the future *Pride of Pittsburg* rained down such heavy blows on the favorite that the referee stopped the fight and awarded McClelland the victory.

His last appearance as an amateur fighter took place in Cleveland, Ohio on May 14 in the intercity tournament in the 115-weight class. His opponent was John Carner (or James Carney as a handwritten document of Jack's names him).

Jack scored a victory by decision in the third round after he knocked Carner down in the second round, who later went on the defense for the remainder of the contest.

Nothing is known about his life for the remainder of '95. One can speculate that he worked and worked out but the sources are silent. In just nine months from his last fight, the same amount of time a child is in utero; Jack would enter the world as a professional fighter in one of Allegheny City's most iconic and now lost buildings, The Cyclorama Hall.

1896

The Cyclorama of the Battle of Gettysburg, or more simply put, the Cyclorama Building or Cyclorama Hall once stood at the corner of Beech Street and Irwin Avenue (modern day Brighton Road). Today nothing of this structure remains. However, if we go back into the historic record one can find a unique form of entertainment and imagine what it would be like to visit the site.

Built in 1887 by the Pittsburgh Cyclorama Company, the three-story building housed an exhibit that gave the viewer the experience of standing near the center front line of the Union Army on July 3 1863 during Pickett's Charge. The drama unfolding along the walls surface shocked visitors who paid .50 to experience the horrors of war. Wax mannequins and other effects added to the experience. Opening day had General Jacob Bowman, a resident of Beech Street, in attendance. He shared his experience along with explaining the exhibit to those that cared to listen. The exhibit stuck around for a year. In 1888, the Cyclorama became a place for dances, political rallies, religious services, and boxing.

Fast forward to 1896 and we find the Cyclorama hosting a return intercity bout between Pittsburg and Cleveland. Jack

McClelland entered the ring on March 4, 1896 and scored a victory over local "colored" fighter, Jim Othello (also known as Kid Othello or Young Othello).

His next fight was against William Kennedy on March 5 with both fighters weighing in at 120. Kennedy, described as lanky, towering over McClelland, *"with owning a wicked eye and a mighty punch"*, fought four rounds to a decision that went to Jack. Even though Kennedy was a skilled dodger, in the third and fourth rounds he could not escape Mac's uppercuts.

On April 14 at the Carnegie Athletic Club, Jack *The Pride of Pittsburg* McClelland entered the ring for the first time as a professional fighter (though his previous fights in '96 are now counted as part of his professional career). All one had to do was declare it to make it so and one's status would change. What makes this so controversial was Jack put himself at odds with the law. While amateur boxing was acceptable and legal, declaring oneself a pro was not. From this point forward, Jack would be entering into an occupation filled with the ever-present threat of police raids and imprisonment.

Jack fought in the preliminary match to the Leonard-Parry main event against a previous opponent, Tommy Mitchell, who he lost to the year before. The contest went six rounds but the sources are conflicting as to the outcome. Some claim that McClelland won while others claim that there was no decision (this is not uncommon, as the reader will see throughout this book).

During the late nineteenth century, fights were not always held in the most conventional of locations like athletic clubs or opera houses. Depending on circumstances such as who was in office, the legal standing of boxing, or who's palms didn't get greased, fights took place in barns, in the woods, or on barges anchored in rivers. On April 23, 1896, Jack and an unknown pugilist named H. Farhion fought on a flat bottom barge out on the Ohio, downriver enough as to be out of the Pittsburg Police's jurisdiction. The fight went nine rounds to a draw. Jack ended up hurting his hand in the final round, which kept him out of boxing for the next six months.

The historical record goes silent until October of 1896. On October 5, the backers of Jack McClelland went to the offices of the *Pittsburg Post* to cover the $25 deposit put down by the backers of Tommy Smith, a featherweight fighter from Chicago. Smith's backers were from Lawrenceville, PA. Jack wanted the fight to go either five, fifteen, or twenty-five rounds with a 115 ringside weigh-in. The fighters would each put up $250 dollars for a purse of $500 going to the winner. The two were set to meet again in the *Pittsburg Post* offices on October 10 to work out the details and sign articles. The details of that meeting are unclear as the backers of Smith posted in the October 17 issue of the *Pittsburg Post* that they would allow their man to fight McClelland at 118. The two parties were set to meet again that night at the *Post's* offices to work out final details. Later on October 20, the two fighters agreed to fight on November 16 within one hundred miles of Pittsburg; the location kept a secret in fear of a police raid. Both fighters put up the $250 dollars and agreed to five-ounce gloves in a sixteen-foot ring following the Marquis of Queensberry rules. Both boxers were to weigh in at 118 at ringside.

The exact location of the fight is still a mystery today. One source states that it took place in a barn in front of ninety people somewhere eight miles outside of Pittsburg but goes into no further detail, while another places the fight in Wilkinsburg. This would be the most written about of Jack's fights in the year 1896. The *Pittsburg Post* chronicled the fight in incredible detail, giving the reader a blow-by blow description of the action. The fight went six rounds with Jack winning on count of a foul by Smith. During the sixth round, Jack dodged a wicked swing from Smith but tripped and became hung up in the ropes at the edge of the ring. By the rules set forth in in the prefight negotiations, Smith should have allowed Jack to free himself but instead he swung on McClelland with his left, which resulted in a foul, and a victory for *The Pride of Pittsburg*. Jack collected the $500 in addition to a division of the gates receipts. This would be his biggest pay off in his career thus far.

For the remainder of November, 1896 one finds lots of activity in the press about Jack McClelland. Smith's fans say that their man could beat Jack in a rematch and that each fighter should put up $500 dollars this time. This rematch, which was to be in January of 1897 never took place. Smith decamped and took off leaving his backers out $175 and training costs.

Another match that never came into fruition in 1896 was a proposed battle with Paddy McGrath (although the two would box the following year). McGrath, a pugilist from Woods Run, stated in the press that he would fight the winner of the McClelland-Smith contest. Negotiations involving everything from weight to purse began on November 20 and lasted through November 30. The fight never materialized due to weight issues. Jack's camp wanted 115 while the McGrath's people wanted 118. McClelland compromised by offering to split the difference at 116 ½ at weigh-in but McGrath's people would not agree to this, thus dissolving the match. This would be the last well-documented mention of a bout in 1896.

At the close of the year, we find Jack giving a demonstration of Indian Clubs at Bill Corcoran's Wood Street Gym on December 15. There is a conflicting story in the *Pittsburg Press* that states Jack and Jimmy Conlon went four rounds in an exhibition fight that night with Joe Leonard giving the demonstration. With lax fact-finding and word of mouth reporting, papers during this period sometimes print conflicting accounts of the same event. What really happened that night on Wood St will forever remain a mystery.

Just before the end of the year on December 22, Jack makes one last appearance before the holidays at the Bedford Athletic Club. The *Pittsburg Post* states that Mac fought in a match with one-minute rounds. The opponent and the outcome are both lost to time as the sources fall silent. With that, the year comes to a close.

1897

The year dawned with a challenge from Paddy McGrath. McGrath challenged Jack in '96 only to have it fall through over a weigh-in dispute. This time the two were set to go on February 9. However, blood poisoning kept McGrath from making that fight date. The two would meet later in the year.

While Jack would not meet any contenders for money in the first month of the New Year, he continued to train at Corcoran's Gym on the third floor of 515 Wood Street. Jack took on Alex Tracey of North Adams at Corcoran's on January 23 in a *"lively set"* as the *Pittsburg Post* puts it. This would be his only recorded time in the ring in January but again, there was no prize money at stake.

Jack was becoming a rising star in the boxing world and his opinion of other fighters, even those not in the same weight class, mattered. On February 8, the *Chicago Tribune* ran an article in the sports section asking Jack's opinion on the upcoming Corbett-Fitzsimmons fight. Jack was of the opinion that Fitzsimmons, who he said was the stronger and harder hitter of the two, would be victorious. His prediction came true when Fitzsimmons sent

Corbett down to the mat with his *"solar plexus"* punch in the fourteenth round.

On February 9, McGrath's men told the *Pittsburg Post* that he was healed and ready to face *The Pride of Pittsburg* in two weeks. The two sides were to meet on February 11 to sign the articles but Mac and his team were a no-show as they were on route to Niles, Ohio to fight Squirrel Finnerty. The McGrath-McClelland bout was again in limbo.

The Finnerty-McClelland match in Niles, Ohio turned out to be Jack's first recorded run in with the law. The sport of boxing was not universally legal across the nation. The reasons for this predominantly revolved around the idea that the sport attracted the worst kind of people and that it promoted sin and vice. Particular cities with specific religious groups or temperance movements would boycott the fight or force the hand of city officials to shut it down. The lawfulness of boxing depended on who was in office in any particular year both on the local and state level. This lead to the fighters risking jail time if they decided to fight in an area that outlawed the sport. If you were determined to fight in specific cities, you did so clandestinely. In this particular instance, the exact location of the fight was kept secret so as to avoid police interference. However, it appears to have taken place along the Mahoning River. With very little in the way of eyewitness accounts, the sources only state that it was a bitter fight for the first five rounds with Jack being the better of the two. The sixth round started around midnight. That is when pandemonium broke loose. When Sheriff Berry of Trumbull County and his men came through the door, they had guns drawn. Squirrel, who had previously spent time in jail for prizefighting, fled the scene by jumping out a window and swimming to the opposite shore. He was arrested one hour later. Jack was hustled out of the building and to safety. However, his brother, William, found himself in jail for the night. The Mayor of Niles, who attended, told the Sheriff that he had permission to host the fight. Many prominent men who came out to watch the bout met the same fate as William. Those that escaped started a stamped with one reporter being knocked down. The winner of the fight by decision was Mac.

Back in Pittsburg on February 17, the two sides representing

McGrath & McClelland finally signed the articles for a bout in March. In the meantime, Mac was supposed to fight a man by the name of John McNulty in Braddock on the twenty-fifth but McNulty had to back out as he cut the tip of one of his fingers off in an accident. McClelland's old amateur opponent Jack Kinlow, who had embarked on his own professional career and was making quite the name for himself, volunteered to step in take McNulty's place. Jack refused on the grounds that he had trained to fight McNulty and no one else. However, he would be willing to meet in a finish fight after the McGrath match.

With March came the match that was almost a year in the making. McGrath and Mac met on the twelfth to select a referee and then again on the fourteenth to finalize the details of the fight which was to go twenty rounds. Both sides were ready to slug it out to see who the better man was. In the days leading up to the battle between these two popular featherweights, the newspapers ran articles, which included boasts from each boxer. The *"sports"* were whipped up into a shark like feeding frenzy. They were ready for blood.

In the late nineteenth century the German Maennerchor (translation: Men's Choir) Club, located in McKee's Rocks hosted fights to help pay for the cost of the building. On March 16, Mac and McGrath would settle once-and-for-all who the better boxer was. The event was oversold so people were sneaking through the windows and the chaos was such that boxer, George Finley, took a bullet to the arm from a guard for reasons lost to time.

At 10:30 PM, the fighters entered the ring. McGrath got the ovation over Mac. In Jack's corner was manager Billy Corcoran (who may have been Jack's brother-in-law) and Billy Cameron. The two fighters weighed in, Mac at 115 and McGrath at 113. Both went to their corners and waited for the bell.

From the outset it was a one sided fight with Mac dominating the boxer from Woods Run. The first two rounds Mac had McGrath groggy from an onslaught of punches. McGrath's friends who cheered as he entered the ring were now silent as their champion took a beating. The third round started and it looked as if McGrath came out of the corner fresh but it was all Mac again. He hit McGrath repeatedly in the face as Paddy staggered but still managed to keep to his feet. Then Mac hit him right in the jaw sending McGrath to the mat. He remained on the floor for a nine count and got back up but Jack rushed him and sent Paddy back to the canvas with more lethal blows. McGrath got up but it was clearly over. He was leaning on the ropes with Jack raining down blows on his head. Finally, his second threw in the sponge and the fight was over. In three rounds, Jack had made $650 ($500 side bet/ $150 purse). In the March 18 edition of the *Post*, the writer states that $3,000 exchanged hands in bets on the McGrath-McClelland fight.

On March 31, Mac made his one and only trip to Manhattan to take on Charles Leopold at the New York Athletic Club. From the start, it was all Mac again. One paper describes how Mac used Leopold as a human punching bag, another as a human chopping block. The *Pittsburg Post* stated by the eighth round Leopold's chest and face were covered in blood. To his credit though, he never gave up, going the full ten rounds. The decision went to Mac. Leopold refused to shake his hand at the end.

April brought with it a new challenger, a fighter from Pittsburgh's Lawrenceville neighborhood who, according to his friends *"hit like a sledge hammer"*. That pugilist was Pat Murphy. For the better part of the month, it was back and forth between the two trying to meet to sign the articles. Both had agreed to weigh-in at Corcoran's Gym the day of the fight at 3:00 PM to make sure both were at 118. The bout would take place on April 21 in Carnegie, PA. At 10 PM both fighters entered, Murphy got the applause but Jack got the win.

From the outset of the first round, Murphy lived up to his reputation as a swinger. That is to say, he just took wild swing after wild swing. He rushed Mac around the ring, whipping wild haymakers, looking for that knockout punch, an approach that only served to tire him out quickly. The second round started the same as the first but this time Jack took the initiative, knocking Murphy down twice. Mac dominated the third round and knocked Murphy down to the canvas four times, the last sending him into dreamland.

A few days later on April 26, Mac and Murphy would meet socially and chat, but the subject of boxing was never broached.

On May 1, Jack would once again fight on a flat bottom barge, this time anchored off Woods Run. There really is not much information out there about this event save that it was a low-key affair that resembled more of a family party with food and drink. Three matches took place that day. Mac knocked out Bob Black in the third round. His brother, William McClelland, fought that day against Ed Williamson. No outcome of the latter fight exists today in print.

On June 3, Jack boxed an impromptu bout against Loudon Campbell in Braddock, PA, even though he was not on the bill. When main eventers Jack Kinlow and Elmer Morgan refused to fight due to low funds in the house (due to poor attendance), Campbell, who was there working as Morgan's second, decided to appease the disappointed crowd by announcing that he would fight any man present at 130. When no one responded, Jack leapt up onto the stage and agreed to fight. The two boxed for six rounds to a draw. In Jack's private notes concerning his fight career, there is no mention of this dust up.

Henry Mason, an African-American fighter from Scottdale had been making cracks for a while about Mac saying that *The Pride of Pittsburg* would not fight him at 120 and insisting on 113. Mac went to the *Pittsburg Post's* office and deposited a $25 in lieu of a forfeit telling Mason to do the same. This would be the only action for Mac in the month of July.

At the Kittanning Opera House on August 24 (another paper lists the 27th), Mason quit in the third round (another paper says the fifth) stating that his hands were sore. The Kittanning "sports" thought Mason faked the injury because he could not take the punishment from McClelland. Mason threw out a challenge at the end saying he would like to fight Jack again down the line. Mac said he would oblige if Mason found backers. They would fight again in 1900.

In October of 1897, the rumblings of a Kinlow-McClelland match began to appear in the papers, though the fight would not happen until early the following year. Another fight, this time against Yock Henniger was to take place on November 15. The articles were signed on October 31 but the fight fell through due to Yock's busy schedule in New York at the time. In November, Mac would take on one of the toughest fighters on the East Coast, Joe Bernstein.

Joe Bernstein, also known as the "Bowery Champ" hailed from the Lower Eastside of Manhattan. This Jewish boxer would become one of the best featherweights of the era, taking on world champions George Dixon, Terry McGovern, Young Corbett II, Solly Smith, and Dave Sullivan.

Bernstein arrived in Pittsburg on November 9. Within the next few days, both parties made deposits and scheduled the fight for November 22. In the meantime, Jack performed at a benefit show for Jeff Powers, a fellow boxer at the Allegheny Athletic Club.

At Kenyon Hall in Allegheny City, the "Bowery Champ" and *The Pride of Pittsburg* met to duke it out. The bout was scheduled for eight rounds but the police would only allow four per fight. So in order to get around this the two took a two-minute break after the fourth, came back, and fought the remaining four to a draw.

The papers state that Mac was the better of the two men. However, the articles specified that if they should go the full eight no decision would be given. Both walked away with some bumps and Mac had a bloody nose. The last big thing for Jack in November was signing to fight Fred Fairman on December 9.

Fred Fairman was a carbon setter for the Allegheny Electric Department. Fairman trained hard but an injury caused by a shattered globe, which cut his wrist, ended his chance to fight Mac that year. Fairman approached Mac's people about calling off the fight and taking down his forfeit deposit since the accident was beyond his control. However, Mac's people would not agree to this and said that he either show up to the fight or lose the money. Fairman, who did not want to disappoint his friends agreed he would fight Mac with one hand if needs be. Fairman's trainer, Joe Leonard would hear nothing of this and agreed to step in and fight Mac himself, which Jack gladly accepted as long as Fairman was at ringside.

On December 9 at Kenyon Hall, Mac and Leonard duked it out for four rounds (scheduled for eight but cut short by Captain

Thornton and the police). The sources say the two were evenly matched for rounds one and two but after that, it was all McClelland. He won by decision in the fourth round.

The remainder of the year involved another benefit show and more back and forth between Kinlow and Jack. Mac's career and reputation were on the rise. He had taken on some tough fighters both locally and abroad. However, unknown to McClelland, one of the two toughest fights of his career loomed on the horizon. On a barge on the Ohio, Mac would participate in one of the most talked about events in nineteenth century Pittsburgh boxing history.

1898

On the night of January 13, a large crowd gathered at the Millvale Opera House to witness *The Pride of Pittsburg* take on the Saint-Paul Kid, Jimmy Kennard. No play-by-play of the fight exists in the sources but two papers did record fragmentary pieces of the match within their articles. The *Saint-Paul Globe* states that Kennard knocked Jack down with a blow to the neck in the fifth round. The *Pittsburg Post* records that in the sixth, Kennard knocked Jack down but the latter quickly got back to his feet. Below is a direct quote from the *Pittsburg Post* from the February 3, 1918 edition:

"The Kid was a tough little fellow, and in the sixth round, knocked Mac down. The latter regained his feet in a hurry and began to pummel the Kid unmercifully. In the ninth round, the men flew at each other like savages, and when Kennard was knocked to the floor, the spectators jumped on their seats and yelled ferociously. The Kid got up, and Mac went after him rough-shod. The spectators, still standing on their chairs, swung their hats and screamed in brutish abandon.

The burgess of Millvale, after a hard struggle, managed to jump into the ring and put a sudden stop to the slaughter. Mac was declared the winner."

One week later on the 20th Mac was at the McKeesport Lyceum to face local boxer, Mike Tunney. The fight was supposed to last ten rounds but Mac sent his opponent to the mat in the fourth with a blow to the stomach and a *"clip to the ear"*.

In February, the papers began to report on a possible Eddie Gardner-Jack McClelland match to take place within the near future. This bout would not manifest until April. In the meantime, Mac took on Johnny Lavack in Millvale on February 28.

Hailing from Cleveland, Ohio Lavack fought some of the greats from his era such as Oscar Gardner, Kid Broad, Joe Bernstein, and many others. The description of Lavack's fighting style was that of a rusher who delivered hard blows.

In the first round, Jack is sent down to the mat with a push but gets right back up. The bout goes the full ten rounds to a draw.

Very little in the ways of description can be found save for Mac being knocked down three times and the papers reporting a very tame final round. Unbeknownst to Jack, his next fight would take on a legendary status, bordering on myth.

The Ohio River forms at the Point in Pittsburgh where the Monongahela and the Allegheny converge. Its waters have long been the desire of nations and a highway of commerce linking Southwestern Pennsylvania with the markets of New Orleans. The river also offered a place to anchor offshore and hold prizefights out of the jurisdiction of Pittsburg Police, as long as you were downriver from the city.

On March 12, a flat-bottomed barge departed from Water and Ferry St in Pittsburg and anchored off Neville Island in a secluded cove, adjacent to the back channel and near the bridge that connected the island with Montour Junction in Coraopolis. This remote location would be the site of the match that Jack later claimed was the toughest fight of his career. Tickets were limited to 100 at a price of $10 a ticket (close to $300 in 2017). Two of Pittsburg's best featherweights, Yock Henniger and Jack

McClelland would square off in a bout that only seventy lucky spectators were fortunate enough to witness. Both fighters wore four-once gloves and each put on a clean fight according to one paper. However, if it had not been for a compromise this fight might never have gotten underway.

Both boxers were on the barge with their seconds. In Henniger's corner are Buck Cornellus, Loudon Campbell, Jerry Friel, Joe Bernstein, and Harry Steele. In Mac's, his brother William, Otto Black, Jack Bennett and Jess Pavey. In addition, one paper lists Toby McCurry also in the McClelland camp. The fight should have started at 11 AM. However, Mac would not budge. His refusal was predicated on "*if hitting with one armed free was allowed*". According to the book "*Boxing*" by David Chapel Hutchison:

"*When boxing under rules that require clean breaking, that forbid holding with one hand and hitting with another, there is no risk of coming out of the clinch, but when boxing under 'one arm free' rules which allow hits with one free hand great care must be exercised to keep your hold on your advisory's hands until you are well back."*

Twenty-five minutes passed. Both sides unwilling to budge on the issue. Finally, with a flip of the coin, Mac won out and the fight began. *"It was hard and rapid from start to end,"* stated one paper.

Round one began with both men feeling each other out for a few seconds then Yock rushed McClelland, hitting Jack's body with both fists, and then ducking a right swing. This is how much of the fight went. Yock would lead, doing twice the work of McClelland. Even though that was the case, a source states that he was the fresher of the two and might have won the fight had it gone to a finish.

In the fourth round, Yock drew first blood with a blow to Jack's nose, which began running like a faucet. The fifth was all Yock again. In the seventh, Mac went down for an eight count. By the eighth Mac's sides were glowing red from the onslaught of punches from the West End boxer. In the same round, Yock hit Mac right in the jaw with a wicked punch that must have felt like a freight train colliding with his face. In the eleventh, it was Mac's turn to draw blood, though Yock's seconds claimed Mac used his elbow to bloody their man's nose. In the fifteenth, Yock chased Mac around the ring and hit him with several lefts, which made the audience cheer. In the eighteenth, it was all Mac again. In the twenty-ninth, Mac went down from a blow to the head but got up at the count of six. In the thirtieth, Mac landed three hits to Yock that *"made him see stars"*. By the thirty-fifth round both fighters had run out of gas and the referee dropped the white handkerchief declaring it a draw. Years later, Jack mentioned this bout in an interview with the *Pittsburgh Sun-Telegraph*:

"Henninger (sic) gave me my hardest fight. He really had the better of it. I was a shuffler and the cracks in the flooring bothered me while Yock picked up his feet and moved nimbly about. I later knocked him out in six rounds in Carnegie but in that first fight Yock really made it tough for me."

Later in the interview, he stated that:

"I had him going for a while and his friends wanted him to quit in the 22nd round, but he rallied and carried on until the bout was

stopped and declared even. We fought with four-ounce gloves and received $133 apiece."

Just sixteen days after the punishing thirty-five round, two hour and twenty-five minute fight Mac was back in the ring at the Bedford Athletic Club for a benefit show. His first bout was against Johnny Beers, who was making his pro debut. Mac said he could take him in four rounds. The match lasted three instead with the crowd begging the ref to stop the fight. Beers landed a punch to Mac's face in the second and that is all it took for him to unleash the fury of the Irish on the rookie. Mac showed no mercy and pummeled Beers to win by decision.

The following day on March 29, Mac fought George Engel. Engel would become a very big player in the boxing game in his later career. He managed Pittsburgh greats like Frank Klaus, Harry Greb and even served as best man at the wedding of Steelers owner Art Rooney. Again the fight was stopped in the third, this time by the police who though Engel took enough of a beating. The decision again went to Jack.

Roughly, sixty miles south-west of Pittsburgh is Wheeling, West Virginia. Though technically part of the south, these two cities have much in common. Wheeling and Pittsburgh were and still are working class towns forged from the fires of industry. In addition, just like Pittsburgh, multiple racial and ethnic groups made up the labor force and segregated themselves into neighborhoods. Many of these young guys turned to boxing and produced an exciting scene in *Nail City*.

Eddie Gardner, who fought out of the Metropolitan Club located in the Fulton neighborhood of Wheeling, was to be Jack's next opponent. Both men would weigh in at 120. Depending on the source; Gardner was the favorite on April 3 while the odds were in favor of Jack come fight night on April 4. One hundred Pittsburg fans made the trip to Wheeling to cheer on Mac and even offered 10 to 7 odds to the Wheeling "sports". There were no takers and wisely so. For the first seven rounds, it was an even bout. During the eighth round, Jack drew first blood. From the ninth until the fourteenth both pugilists were dead even again but one hit to the jaw by Mac sent Gardner's chances of winning into a tailspin.

He never recovered from that blow. In the nineteenth, he went down three times. Gardner, shoved against the ropes went down for the first time. When he got up, he received a jab to the face, went down for a nine count, and got up at the last second. That was all Mac needed and he rained down blows on Gardner. This was the end of the match. One source states that Eddie's face looked severely punished while Jack did not appear to have been in a fight at all.

Twenty-one days later, Jack was in Homestead, Pennsylvania to take on Jack Kinlow. Starting back in 1897, there had been a back and forth between Kinlow and McClelland in the papers. Kinlow was eager to fight but the timing was never right. Kinlow even called out Mac saying that McClelland was putting other fighters first and that he was ready at any weight to take on *The Pride of Pittsburg.* On April 25, he got his chance.

The newly open Manhattan Athletic Club wanted to make a name for itself as a club where the noble sport flourished under the Marquis of Queensberry rules, meaning that the fighters adhered to a set of rules that prevented the match from becoming a brawl. The

Kinlow-McClelland bout was the opening night headliner at the Opera House in Homestead. Tickets ranged from $1 to $3 for reserve seats. That night there were eight-hundred people in attendance to watch Kinlow and McClelland duke it out for $250 a side and a $300 purse. Both boxers weighed in at 122 that evening.

At 9:31 PM, Kinlow entered the ring followed by McClelland. The sources do not offer a play-by-play of this fight but they do record that during the third round Mac drew first blood when he hit Kinlow in the face with a full right. They also mention that in the seventh that Kinlow was groggy and went down for a nine count. Though Jack was always on the verge of ending the bout, the gong saved the McKeesport fighter each time. The match went the full fifteen and the decision went to Mac.

There really was not much in the ways of action during the month of May save for a benefit bout against Jimmy Marshall in Washington, PA. The event looming on the horizon was a return to Wheeling. This time to take on Oscar Gardner, also known as "The Omaha Kid", the brother of Eddie whom Jack defeated in April. Though the articles were not signed until June there was enough back and forth in the paper to suspect this match was going to happen. All that was holding up the fight was the compensation. In the end, both agree to fight for sixty-five percent of the gate.

Born in Minneapolis, Minnesota in 1872, Oscar Gardner had a reputation for delivering murderous blows and knocking out opponents with ease. In April of 1898, he fought George Stout in Columbus, Ohio and hit him so hard on his chin in the twelfth round that the man never regained consciousness and died the following morning in the hospital. Gardner was charged with manslaughter but acquitted.

On June 30 at 10 o'clock, Oscar walked through the ropes with buckets, bottles, and other ringside paraphilia. The two would go twenty rounds at 122. From the outset, both fighters put on a great show for the mixed audience of Wheeling and Pittsburg fans. The July 1, 1898 edition of the *Wheeling Intelligencer* gives a blow-by-blow account of the match. The paper paints a picture of an even contest until the tenth round when Gardner lands a blow to Mac's stomach and sends him backwards to the mat. The referee counted to ten and that was it. Mac needed assistance back to his corner.

This was his first loss since 1895. Some of the Pittsburg fans cried *"foul"*. Their claim was that Gardner hit him with a low blow. After an examination by a doctor on site, the count stood and Oscar Gardner became the first man in Jack's professional career to lay him out for a ten count.

The sources are silent during the months of July and August. There is a mention of Jack taking on an unknown at the Bedford A.C. during conclave week (September 15) but nothing beyond that. The results of the match or if it took place at all are lost to time. It is not until October that we find Jack back in the ring. This time against the boxer, that took him thirty-five rounds to a draw, Yock Henniger. No detailed information is available about this fight save that, it took place on October 20 in Carnegie and that Jack took him in six rounds. According to the sources, Yock was ill before the fight. In fact on November 11 Red Mason, who would become Jack's manager later in his career, put together a benefit show for Yock. The West End boxer would be out for the next ten months. Jack participated in the benefit held in the neighborhood of Esplen.

His opponent was "The Ann Arbor Mystery", George Johnson. In a scheduled ten round match, Jack ended it in two with a straight right to the jaw. Yock would go on to recover and meet Jack in 1900.

The last match of 1898 took place at the Youngstown Athletic Club on December 5 against Eddie Lenny of Philadelphia. The two fought with eight-ounce gloves (another source says six) to a draw. Mac describes Eddie as a sprinter, and with a 22 square foot ring; he had plenty of room to move. One thousand people watched the fight. The sources describe it as a vicious back and forth. Jack received an injured left hand and a bloody nose in the eighth while Lenny's body by the fourteenth looked to be showing signs of punishment.

For the remainder of the year Jack found himself in a back-and-forth in the papers with Luke Stevens of Buffalo, NY and as a second for George Lehrman on December 26. This wraps up the year for *The Pride of Pittsburg*. With 1899 days away, Jack vanishes from the record until after the New Year.

1899

At the start of 1899, Mac once again found himself back at the Manhattan Athletic Club in Homestead, this time taking on Luke Stevens. The two had been going back-and-forth in the papers during the latter part of 1898. However, the fight did not materialize until January 13. The boxer from Buffalo and *The Pride of Pittsburg* found themselves in front of a packed house with Loudon Campbell as the referee. This match would be one of many in 1899 that had a bizarre twist. In the February 3, 1918 edition of the *Pittsburgh Post* the writer, John H. Gruber presents this summary of the bout:

"Mac and Luke Stevens of Buffalo, met in a fight that pleased and excited the large attendance until the thirteenth round, when one of Steven's seconds ran into the ring and declared his man's arm was broken. The chief of police followed the second into the ring, while the spectators howled and roared. Of course, Mac got the decision. A doctor, who was said to have been "planted" by the Steven's crowd, followed the chief of police into the ring, examined the arm and nodded his head solemnly in the affirmative."

The sources are silent on the validity of the doctor's diagnosis or his presumed collusion with the Stevens' camp. What happened one hundred and eighteen years ago will remain a mystery. In the *Pittsburg Press*, the following day there is mention that Stevens returned to Buffalo on January 14. A doctor there diagnosed his arm as "*badly wrenched*", and that Stevens would be out of the fight game for several weeks. He claimed he wanted to box Mac again but there was never a rematch.

After the fight with Stevens, the sources place Mac at two benefit shows held at the Bedford Athletic Club located at 52-54 Enoch St in the Hill District of Pittsburgh. Mac even managed one of the events with Loudon Campbell on January 27. As January ended, a new opponent came onto the scene. His name was Tommy Hogan. This would be another strange challenger for *The Pride of Pittsburg*.

Tommy Hogan's hometown is a bit of a mystery. Different sources place him in either Pittsburg or Chicago. Tommy and Jack were originally supposed to fight in Wilkinsburg but the venue could not accommodate. The fight was then moved to a brand new club named The National Athletic Club located in either McKees Rocks or Esplen (it is unclear where exactly it was located. The papers state that it was along the train line fifteen minutes from Market Square and that its location was in one of the two aforementioned neighborhoods). Joe Harris, the owner of the new club went all out and created a fight venue that included comfortable, elevated seats so that everyone had a good view of the action. The Hogan-McClelland fight was the main event for opening night. The two were set to fight twenty rounds for a $350 purse and sixty percent of the gate receipts.

At 9:30 PM on February 13, the fight began with Hogan acting as the aggressor. In fact, this would be the story for the first ten rounds. In the eleventh, the wind shifted and it was all Mac. This would continue for the next five rounds. Then in the seventeenth round, Jack kicked it up and began to pummel his opponent without mercy. The only thing that saved Hogan each time was the gong. *The Pittsburg Gazette* stated in the February 14 edition that if it had gone for one minute longer in the twentieth, the fight would have been Jacks.

However, it was declared a draw. This did not sit well with both pugilists.

In the following days, there were stories that the two wanted to fight again. This time it would be a fight to the finish in front of a small crowd with each man putting up $500. The friends of both pugilists talked them into holding the fight at the National Athletic Club again because an unsanctioned fight to the finish would be illegal. And besides, both could make more money in a proper venue. Both agreed and their second fight took place on February 24.

In the same ring, with the same referee, two men that disliked each other immensely went back at it for a second time. Both fighters weighed in at 128. This time the fight was all Mac from start to finish. He knocked down Hogan several times but could not knock him out. At the end of the twenty rounds, the fight went to McClelland. The two would never meet in the ring again.

In March, the manager of Jimmy Reeder of Altoona came to Pittsburg looking to set up a match with Jack. However, a fight between the two would not happen until 1905. The following month, Oscar Gardner, the only man to knock out McClelland so far telegrammed Jack to meet him at Union Station in Pittsburg to set up a rematch with Eddie Gardner. Jack approved as long as Oscar granted a rematch upon the defeat of Eddie. Oscar agreed and Eddie and Mac were set for a May bout at the Metropolitan Club in Wheeling, WV. On April 18, Mac acted as the referee in a bout between Oscar Gardner and Joe Hopkins in the aforementioned location. His popularity in *Nail City* was growing.

On May 1, Jack met Eddie Gardner at 124 in the Metropolitan Club. This fight would be another bizarre one for the *The Pride of Pittsburg*. The fight was uneven from the beginning with Mac dominating the entire length of the fight. With one minute left in the final round Oscar jumped in the ring, grabbed Mac's waist to save his brother from the beating he was taking. The name for this action is the *Con McVay Act*. Named after Gentleman Jim Corbett's sparring partner, the *Con McVay Act* is when someone jumps into the ring to get the losing man disqualified. Corbett's second jumped in the ring to save him from a beating by Tom Sharkey, much like Oscar did for his brother.

The referee declared Mac the winner of the bout. After the announcement of the decision, Mac walked over to Oscar and reminded him that they were to meet in two weeks. The rematch between the two would not take place until 1900. The following day the papers stated that Eddie became weaker after the fight and *"had a hemorrhage"*. He started to recover on May 2. The rest of the spring and into summer was quiet for Jack. It was not until August 27 that his next opponent appeared on the scene.

Marty McCue was an old timer from New York City (he later became a fixture in the New York State Legislature in both the upper and lower houses). His manager sent a telegram asking if Jack would meet him in Brooklyn on Sept 2. Mac agreed because it did not interfere with an upcoming fight in Wheeling on September 7. The bout held at the Pelicans Athletic Club in Brooklyn was a twenty round draw. Different sources claim each was the winner. However, the next bout provided a clear victor.

Back in Wheeling, West Virginia at the Metropolitan Club in front of two thousand fans, Jack faced an African-American fighter from New York named Joe Hopkins. A muscular man who looked like Michelangelo chiseled him from stone; Hopkins had an already impressive resume taking on Sam Bolen, Ike "The Belfast Spider" Weir, and Spike Sullivan.

Mac was the favorite between the two because he was taller and had a longer reach. With 5 to 4 and then 5 to 3 odds there were no takers. Both Hopkins and Mac came in under weight for this one (the two set 126 for weigh-in).

For the first two rounds the boxers measured each other up then Mac came out as the aggressor. In the fifth round, Mac had Hopkins going but the bell saved the New Yorker. That was the beginning-of-the-end of the fight. For the remainder of the bout *The Pride of Pittsburg* sent him to the mat numerous times. In the fifteenth round, Hopkins came out of the corner aggressively but it did no good. A left to the stomach and a right to the jaw sent Hopkins down for nine seconds. Then a straight right jab to the chin sent him down again. Hopkins got up one last time. However a left to the stomach and a right to the jaw knocked him out. Mac was victorious.

Jack's next opponent was the former featherweight champion, Solly Smith out of Los Angeles, California. Smith had beaten future hall of fame member, George Dixon in 1897 for the title and lost it a year later to Dave Sullivan. The fight, which took place at the Esplen Borough Hall on October 2, was the most bizarre of Mac's fight schedule for 1899. An air of suspicion hung over the bout. In the fourth round, Mac went down on both knees. The referee began the count. Upon reaching nine, he started all over again for reasons unknown and then made it to eight before Mac got up, making it a seventeen count. The reason for this was and still is a mystery. The twenty round match had an abrupt end in the sixth round when Smith claimed he had been fighting with a broken wrist since the second round. The hall echoed with cries of "*fake*". Members of the audience swore they saw Smith fighting with both hands up to and including round six. No suspicion fell on Mac but Billy Corcoran was quick to defend him in the papers the following day. The exact nature of these events and the validity of the fight remain unknown.

The Cyclorama Hall was the next venue to host one of Mac's

fights. With a three-thousand-person capacity, the November 15 bout drew in two-thousand fight fans. Joe Fairburn of Philadelphia was Jack's opponent. Both fighters weighed in at 122. The ten round match went to Mac by way of points, even though Fairburn's manager claimed it should have been a draw. According to the write-up of the match found in the November 16 edition of the *Pittsburg Press* the fight started out with Fairburn leading. However, from the fourth on it was all Mac. During the sixth round, Jack opened up an old wound above Fairburn's eye and according to the *Pittsburg Press*, "*the claret rolled down Fairburn's face*". Each time Fairburn's second plastered it up, Jack knocked it right back off. At one point, tape that was supposed to help with the wound slid over one of Fairburn's eyes. All of this helped contribute to *The Pride of Pittsburg's* victory.

The last fight of the year for Mac was lackluster according to fans and Mac himself. The fight was against Sam Bolin, an African-American fighter who took on such exceptional pugilists as Marty McCue and Oscar Gardner. The bout took place in Wheeling in front of a very mixed crowd. A delegation of

Pittsburg's "colored" athletes accompanied Bolin via train to Wheeling to cheer him on. The Union Club of Allegheny would later host an event in honor of Bolin upon his return to the *Smokey City* on December 23. The decision for the ten round fight held on December 21 was a draw. However, even the Pittsburg papers said Bolin should have won. Mac ended the year on sour note.

1900

According to the Chinese Zodiac, January 1, 1900 was the *Year of the Pig* but a better name for it would be the *Year of the Rematch*. With the exception of one fighter, Jack would have rematches with former opponents and multiple matches in one year against the same boxers. Jack would also fight more opponents this year than any other. As the year began, Jack found himself gearing up for three fights. The first was against Eddie Santy. This fight never materialized and these two would not meet until 1901. The second was a rematch against Sam Bolin. There was lots of talk about a rematch between the two throughout 1900 but they never set foot in the ring together again. Lastly, there was Kid Broad out of Cleveland. These two would meet twice in 1900 but the first time would not be until May. For the first month of the New Year, Jack had no ring action. All of this would change with a rematch in February.

On February 5, the New Kensington Athletic Club put on a bout between Jack and Henry Mason. These two first met in 1897 in Kittanning with Jack scoring a win. The rematch took place at Arnold Station along the Allegheny Valley Railroad with an 8:30

PM start time. The boxers fought under the Marquis of Queensberry rules. While no complete blow-by-blow of the bout was recorded what little there is states that Jack was too clever and the better hitter. He walked away with the victory. The two would never again meet in the ring.

February 22, Jack was in Utica, NY at the Genesee Athletic Club to take on Billy Ryan. Ryan would hold the distinguished spot of being the most frequently fought opponent in a single year, with four matches between February and December. Ryan was the fan favorite being from the *Empire State*. Mac scored a decision in the twenty-fifth round. The crowd hissed with displeasure. The fans were sure that it was a draw. Even the papers were divided on the issue with some saying that Mac was the better fighter and deserved the win while others say he clearly lost. The Buffalo Evening News said that Ryan outpointed Mac and it should have been a draw while the Buffalo Express said the fight was all McClelland. Ryan said he wanted a rematch within two months. The score was now 1-0 with Mac in the lead.

Paddy Murphy would be the last opponent Jack faced in February. Murphy and Jack had met three years earlier in Carnegie with Mac winning the contest. This time Murphy was ready for him. The fight was held at the Lawrenceville Athletic Club on the corner of Butler and 46 St. This match would be the first in the new club on February 26. Paddy Murphy was a local favorite and ready to redeem himself. Sadly, this did not happen for the Irish fighter. Again, there are no round-by-round commentaries found in the sources and the only mention of the outcome is on the Boxingrec.com website, which states that Murphy was disqualified and the bout awarded to Jack. The validity of the websites claim cannot be verified at the time of writing.

On March 8, there is a post that Tim Callahan and Jack were to fight in private but due to the unlawful nature of the bout, it never happened. The two would not meet until 1904. On March 14, Jack is again at a benefit, this time for Eddie Kennedy. Turner Hall in Allegheny hosted as Mac took on George Engel. The sources describe the match as *"hot and fast"*. The outcome is unknown. On March 16, the only man so far to K.O. Mac, Oscar Gardner, writes that he wants a rematch. The two would meet in July.

On March 30, Jack would find himself once again at the Genesee Athletic Club in Utica, NY. This time his opponent was Jack Hamilton. Hamilton and McClelland would face each other three times before the year was out. Both fighters agreed to 124 and to box under the Marquis of Queensberry rules. Hamilton was the favorite to win. Just before the bout, Billy Ryan challenged Jack to a rematch, which he accepted. The fight was lopsided with Hamilton only having control of the first round with the rest of the fight dominated by McClelland. At the end of the twenty-fifth round, the decision went to Mac who beat Hamilton by points.

With spring came a rematch against Billy Ryan. The fight was originally supposed to be held on April 25 in Syracuse, NY but it had to be moved a day later due to a large Elks convention being held that day downtown. The Monarch Athletic Club put up a thousand dollar purse and offered the two combatants fifty percent of the gate receipts, the winner getting seventy-five percent of that and the loser twenty-five. The boxers agreed to fight under Marquis of Queensberry rules, which means clean breaks with no hitting in the clinch or during the breakaways. The bout was either twenty-three or twenty-five rounds (different sources give different numbers) and the two would weigh-in at 122. Just like the previous fight, the decision was controversial. The sources state that Ryan commanded an incredible lead in the early rounds with Jack trailing. It was not until later in the fight that *The Pride of Pittsburg* mounted a comeback. However, it was too late. Ryan was too far ahead in points. Billy Corcoran, Jack's manager, stated that Ryan did not adhere to the Marquis of Queensberry rules and danced around Jack without engaging him, using his footwork to keep out of danger. Corcoran believed the fight should have went to McClelland. The score was now 1-1. This also marked the beginning of a shaky period in Mac's boxing career.

William M Thomas, also known as Ned Broad or Kid Broad, was Jack's next opponent. Broad was originally from Liskeard, Cornwall in the United Kingdom but resided in Cleveland, Ohio. He was a strong fighter with a powerful punch.

The Business Men's Gymnasium (the former site of the Academy of Music), a venue that could hold three thousand fans (or twenty-five hundred according to another source) hosted the bout on May 1. Mac was about to take on one of the toughest opponents in the featherweight class and the outcome was not good. The fight was to be twenty rounds but it only went thirteen with Kid Broad scoring a knock out. The write-ups of the bout say Broad started out slow but in the twelfth round, he went full throttle and began to pummel Mac. In the final round, Mac clinched repeatedly to save himself and it was apparent he would not finish the round. An uppercut to the jaw sent *The Pride of Pittsburg* to the mat. It appeared to the referee that Mac was out cold so he awarded the fight to Broad. Mac jumped up and said he had nine seconds to rest and protested the decision. This would be his second loss in a row.

The next fight would be a rematch against Jack Hamilton at the Millvale Opera House on June 11 in front of 600 fans. Both fighters appeared to be in top shape, with Mac stating that he wanted to show his Pittsburg fans he was his old self again. The first round started with a swing by Hamilton. Mac ducked and delivered a blow right to the body.

At the end of the first round, Hamilton landed a punch on Jack's jaw as the gong sounded. In the second, Hamilton came out swinging again. Mac dropped down to one knee to avoid being knocked into oblivion. The fight would go on pretty much like this for the twenty rounds. The sources state that it was a very scientific match from start-to-finish. The boxer from Troy, NY was the aggressor for the majority of the bout but Jack was able to avoid his devastating blows. Just as the final round was about to end, Mac landed a left to Hamilton's mouth as the gong sounded. A full play-by-play of the fight is available in the June 12 edition of the *Pittsburg Post*. The referee declared the bout a draw.

The Millvale Opera House was again the venue for another rematch. This time it was against Oscar Gardner, alias "The Omaha Kid". As previously stated, Gardner was the only man before Broad to K.O. Mac. Prior to the fight, Mac trained as he had never trained before and wanted to redeem himself in both the eyes of his fans and himself. The following is from the *Pittsburg Commercial Gazette*. It states that Mac:

"Fought much differently from his previous fights and showed a general improvement all around. Both his footwork and his headwork were excellent and his judgement of distance was somewhat remarkable. During the entire 20 rounds he did not miss more than two blows and only missed those because there was a trickle of blood down into his eye from a cut just above the nose on the forehead."

In the twenty rounds, both men took a beating. Gardner ended the fight with a swollen and cut left eye. Mac on the other hand had a bad cut on his left cheek, a cut on the forehead above the nose, and a badly swollen and discolored left eye. Again, it was a decision. There was some talk of Gardner cheating when in the clinch by throwing some punches but that did not affect the outcome.

On August 9, Mac would have a rematch with Kid Broad in a tent on a ballfield in Millvale at ten o'clock at night. This was a late match, which drew criticism from fans in the papers saying that the start time was too late for most workers to attend. However, that did not stop five thousand people from showing up.

Broad was about to face a different *Pride of Pittsburg*, one that was better prepared to take on the *Forest City* fighter. The *Pittsburg Post* had this to say about Jack:

"McClelland was at his best, and his best is a superb article. His cleverness puzzled Broad at all points, and he had much trouble finding McClelland at all stages of the game. Broad's strength and aggressiveness are alone what saved him, so far as the decision was concerned."

In a strange article in the August 13 edition of the *Pittsburg Post*, it seems there was a warrant out for both Mac and Broad from the Alderman of Allegheny. The exact nature of the offence is not clear other than the two would be charged with assault and battery. However, as the fight did not take place in Allegheny City, one has to wonder what legal footing these warrants rested. It appears that the constable sent to deliver the warrants went to the fight and never delivered them. The article ends with his exact whereabouts a mystery. The article does not hint at foul play but reads more like a man that wished to vanish. The warrants were later dropped with no arrests made.

Jack's next fight was back in *Nail City*, at Fulton Park on September 3 against New York boxer, Tony Moran. The description of Moran was of a stocky Italian who was easily excitable and lacking in any scientific knowledge of the noble sport. This was an easy victory for Mac. The papers state that Moran rushed Jack for the first seven rounds, while *The Pride of Pittsburg* played it cool. From the eighth until the end of the fight in the fifteenth, it was all Mac. He knocked Moran down twice in the fourteenth and in the last round Mac sent him to the mat with a left to the jaw and a right to the ribs. Moran had to be carried back to his corner and according to one write up was *"very sick after the fight"*.

Back in Pittsburg on September 5, Mac was responsible for stopping a fight instead of engaging in one. John Weathers was in handcuffs and being transported on the Central Avenue Street Car to jail for fighting in Alderman Eynon's office above Kirkpatrick St. Weathers is described as a big man about 200 hundred pounds. The constable who arrested him, James T Hardin, was only half his weight at best. While in handcuffs, Weathers said:

"You've got me handcuffed but I can do you anyway."

The next thing Weathers felt was a tap on his should. He turned to see McClelland standing above him. Jack calmly told Weathers:

"You better keep quiet and go along with him."

Weathers must have recognized Mac because he turned around and caused no more trouble.

September 13, Mac was again in Wheeling at the Metropolitan Club to take on Jack Hamilton for the third and final time that year. He won by a decision. He would face Hamilton again in 1901 and again in 1904.

As the leaves began to fall, Jack would face three opponents in the month of October. The first was the man whom he fought on two previous occasions, Yock Henniger. The Millvale Opera House was the scene of this rematch on the 11th. Fans of Henniger claimed that he was back in top shape and ready to even the score with Mac. Alas, this was not to be. The sources say it was even for the first seventeen rounds but for the remaining three it was all Jack. It was clear by the last round that Yock could not defend himself and sunk to the floor for a seven count. Upon getting up Mac rained down blows upon the West End boxer. Mac won by points.

October 20, Mac fought his first match in Canada at the Bijou Theater. The Crescent Club booked a fight between him and Joe Leonard, another rematch in the year of rematches. This was another easy victory for Jack. The fight was supposed to go twenty rounds but it ended in the sixth. During the first round, Jack hit Leonard in the nose, which continued to bleed for the remainder of the fight. In the sixth, Jack hit him in the jaw with a hard right that took all the wind out of Leonard's sails and then began to beat him with both hands at will. Leonard began hitting in the clinch to save himself, which led to the ref stopping the fight, and awarding it to Jack. The consensus was that Leonard would not have made it through that round.

Back on U.S. soil Mac met his last opponent of the month on October 30. Once again, he would take on Billy Ryan. This match produced a low turnout of only three-hundred which one paper blamed it being a presidential election year. In addition, the crowd was not pleased with either fighter this time. The papers state that it was too much of a defensive fight with neither one taking the lead. It was a draw. The score was now 1-1-1 for both fighters.

The last fight of the year was once again Billy Ryan for the fourth and final time of the year, though the two would meet three more times in Jack's career. The fight took place at the Mahoning Club in Youngstown, Ohio and resulted in a draw. This time the sources state that the fight was *"fast and scientific"*. The final tally between these two is 1-1-2.

Again, to summarize the year, with the exception of Tony Moran, each opponent Jack faced was either a rematch from a previous year or someone he fought multiple times during the year. The year ended with the booking of a fight in Windber, Pennsylvania, on News Years day 1901. At the dawn of the twentieth century, the Pittsburg featherweight would take on the welterweight champion of Central Pennsylvania, Jack McKeever.

1901

Located approximately eight miles south of Johnstown, Windber was another hub of industrial activity like many small towns in and around the Pittsburgh area. These working class areas were hotbeds for boxing, producing both fans and fighters alike. Jack McKeever was one of those battlers. A welterweight with a great fighting background, he had beaten the best in the area and was now challenging Jack to a fight on New Year's Day (some sources mistakenly say New Year's Eve).

In the final days of the nineteenth century, there was a lot of buildup in the papers about this event set to take place at the Windber Opera House on January 1. This ten round bout would be at catch weight with Jack coming in at 126 and McKeever at 140. Though the size and weight difference favored McKeever, Mac put him out in three rounds. The January 2 edition of the *Pittsburg Post* had this to say about the fight:

"The first and second rounds were about even, but in the third Mac sailed in and with a punch in the stomach knocked McKeever down. The later (sic) got up and began to claim foul. Mac then gave him a clip on the jaw which knocked him out."

This David vs Goliath match would be the start of a very good year for *The Pride of Pittsburg*. He was in demand as a second for many fights, including one just a few days later on January 4 where he was in the corner of Dave Wayne when he fought George Tucker in a ten round bout in Washington, Pa. However, his next bout harkens back to '99 with it's bizarre twist. Jack almost lost a fight due to the overzealous actions of his second, Otto Black.

At the Millvale Opera House on January 29, Jack would take on Chicago fighter Eddie Santry, a onetime featherweight champion who took on greats like George Dixon, Ben Jordan, Dave Sullivan and Battling Nelson. In front of a large crowd, Jack hit Santry in the stomach and then two to the jaw to K.O. the *Windy City* pugilist. Santry tried to pull himself up by using the ropes on the seven count but fell backwards and was out cold. What made this bout memorable was not the fight itself but the actions of one, Otto Black. The January 30 edition of the *Pittsburg Post* had this to say:

"In the second Corcoran told Jack to sail in at his best and Jack did so, with the result that Santry was doing a lot of guess work and was finally knocked out. McClelland's seconds were so

elated over the turn of affairs that one of them, Otto Black, attempted to jump into the ring. Mike Donovan, tried to hold him back but he went in. Then Corcoran, fearing that the battle would be lost on a foul, made a swipe at Black, knocking him across the ring. Otto fell heavily and when picked up it was discovered that his collar bone was broken. He was tied up by the doctor and sent home. While Black was in the ring, Sentry's second loudly claimed foul, but Referee Bradburn, who was tolling off the count over Santry, failed to notice. In fact, there was so much noise all around that he probably never heard the claim foul."

Some writers claimed that Jack got lucky because Santry was out of shape. Nevertheless, it was another victory for McClelland whose reputation was growing nationwide as a real contender in the featherweight division.

The month of February was quiet, save for Jack acting as a referee in a bout between Harry Lemmons, an African-American fighter from Niagara Falls and Jack Foley of Youngstown. The bout took place in Steubenville, Ohio. There was also talk of Jack heading to England to take on Ben Jordan. However, it was not until March that Mac would enter the ring again.

In the Midwest town of Elwood, Indiana on March 16, Jack fought Willy Fitzgerald of Brooklyn, NY at the Coliseum Athletic Club located on 10th Street. Mac was originally supposed to take on Chicago fighter, Ole Olson. At the last minute, Olson refused to fight for reasons only known to himself so the promoters substituted Fitzgerald. In front of a large audience, Mac scored a win via disqualification. Fitzgerald had Mac going for most of the fight. However, he hit low twice in the ninth round and received a warning from the referee. Later in the fourteenth round, he fouled out. The two would never meet in the ring again.

On Good Friday, April 5, Mac was in Toronto, Canada to take on Ole Olson, the man who refused to fight in Indiana a few weeks earlier. Olson, a ring vet with matches against Battling Nelson and Loudon Campbell, would take on *The Pride of Pittsburg* in front of two-thousand fight fans at the Mutual Street Rink. The fight was one-sided from the beginning with Jack in total control. He chased Olson around the ring. The papers describe Olson's defense as swinging his arms like windmills to avoid a volley of punches raining down on him. This did little as Jack had the height and reach advantage. In the first six rounds, Olson was on the defense. In the seventh, Olson hit Jack in the nose, which started to bleed. In the eighth, Jack knocked Olson down but couldn't finish him off. Nothing much occurred until the thirteenth, though Olson appeared distressed and losing steam. In the sixteenth round, Mac hit Olson in the jaw. One source states, *"He went down like a log, rolling over and over."* Olson recovered but Jack sent him back down to the mat again. When he got up for the third time the ref saw that Olson was in no condition to continue and that was all she wrote. McClellend was awarded the victory. The two would meet again twice in 1902.

Mac suffered his first loss in 1901 to former featherweight champion, Dave Sullivan on April 29 in Louisville, Kentucky. At the Buckingham Theater in front of three-thousand people, Mac had Sullivan going for the majority of the fight and it looked as if *The Pride of Pittsburg* was going to pull off another win. However, in the twelfth round of a twenty-five round fight it all unraveled for

McClelland. This quote comes from the April 30 edition of the *Pittsburg Post:*

"In the twelfth both came up apparently fresh. McClelland lead off with a right swing. Sullivan clinched and stepping back, upper cut him twice, then led a hard right, which sent McClelland to the floor for eight seconds. McClelland got up and clinched, Sullivan trying again to get in the knock-out blow. McClelland landed right and left lightly. Sullivan then upper cut him twice, landing left, crossed with a right and McClelland was out, falling heavily on the floor, his head striking first."

This was Jack's only loss of 1901 though it was a bitter one. He would never have a chance to settle the score as he and Sullivan never fought again.

From May through July, there was very little activity in the McClelland camp. On May 13 there was supposed to be a bout between Mac and Eddie Gardner in Wheeling before the anti-boxing laws took effect on the 15th. However, this never occurred.

In June, there was a man claiming to be Jack McClelland in the

Monongahela Valley. The imposter was booked to fight Lawrence Lutz in Brownsville, PA. However, when the police discovered that the man was not who he claimed to be they ran him out of town. Jack put an announcement in the *Pittsburg Press* that he would like to meet the pretender. At the time of writing for this book no information about his identity or what became of him can be located.

There was ongoing talk about matching up Mac and Tim Callahan in Bridgeport, CT but by July 29, the deal was dead-in-the-water. Lack of money was the reason given for the termination of the bout. The two would not meet until 1904.

In the final month of summer 1901, Billy Corcoran decided to put this announcement in the *Pittsburg Press* on August 11:

"I will match McClelland to meet Dave Sullivan, Kid Broad, or the champion, Terry McGovern. I will also match Mike Donovan to meet anyone in his class, including Joe Wolcott, Mathews, or the champion Rube Ferns, the contests to take place after McClelland and Donovan's contests Aug 21 and 22, at Kittanning. The challenge is open to anyone, of the top notch boxers, and if none of

them will accept McClelland and Donovan will meet any two local boxers and give the entire receipts to the striking steel workers."

Permission was asked to stage a bout between Donovan and McClelland at White's Opera House in McKeesport with all proceeds going to the striking workers but Mayor Robert J Black denied the request.

Mac was back in the ring against Eddie Gardner on August 21 at the Kittanning Opera House. The twenty round match, fought at 125 under Marquis of Queensberry rules was a draw. Neither man got into position to deliver the knockout blow. The rounds were back and forth with each boxer winning one and losing the next. Boxrec.com has Jack marked as a win for this bout but the primary source evidence contradicts this claim. This would be the last time these two would meet in the ring with Jacks record being 2-0-1.

There was talk in October about bringing *The Pride of Pittsburg* out to Chicago for a rematch against Ole Olson but it never got off the ground. However, Mac would fight two men at the beginning of 1902 in the *Windy City*.

Jack Hamilton would be the last opponent of the year for Mac. The fight was supposed to take place at the Twentieth Century Club in Detroit, MI on November 21, 1901 but it was relocated to New Castle, PA at the Opera House for the same day. The Women's Christian Temperance Union wanted to stop the fight and went to see Mayor Warnock. However, he was out of town at the time. The fight went on much to the chagrin of the W.C.T.U. The fifteen rounds ended in a draw but Jack was hurt during the bout. The exact nature of the injury is unknown but it prevented him from fulfilling his obligation to fight Tim Callahan in Canada on Thanksgiving Day. *The Pride of Pittsburg* would go into recovery and he would not fight again until February of 1902.

1902

If 1900 was the *Year of the Rematch* then 1902 could be called the *Year of the Draw*. Out of nine fights, seven resulted in a draw. That is 77.7% rounded up to 78%. 1902 would also be the last year Billy Corcoran managed Jack. The year would begin with a brief mention on January 19 that after three months off, though the actual time was fifty-nine days give or take, that Jack was back in training at Corcoran's Wood St. Gym. His first match of the year would take place far away from the *Smokey City*, in the land of the Columbian Exposition and the Hay Market Riot.

On February 2, the *Pittsburg Press* stated that Jack was back in shape and ready to take on any contender in his weight class. It did not take long. Within seventeen days, he was in Chicago to face off against Eddie Santry, an opponent he defeated the previous year at the Millvale Opera House. When Jack arrived in Chicago, the paper, *Inter Ocean* quoted him as saying:

"*I am here to meet anyone of my size. I would like to box Olson, Ryan, O'Keefe, Mowatt, Sullivan, and Broad in that succession, and will do my best to whip them all. If Broad will come down to my weight, I will risk a handy piece of coin that I can thrash his head off. The one man I would like to meet is Benny Yanger, but I don't suppose the weights could be arranged, although he wants to fight Broad, and Broad is far bigger than I am."*

That same night, the Acme Athletic Club put on a bout at Brand's Hall, once located at 164 North Clark Street on Chicago's North Side, featuring McClelland and Santry. The six round bout would be the first draw of the year for *The Pride of Pittsburg*. According to the sources, the crowd was small but the fight was good. Depending on which source you choose to believe Santry held his own for either the first three or four rounds but was always on the defense, while Mac went after him with all he had. By the fifth, Mac had him against the ropes or in the corners smashing away at leasure. Santry's defense was just to cover up and run out the clock. He did try some offensive blows with jabs to Mac's face but they had little effect. When the gong rang at the end of the sixth, Mac was not able to deliver the knockout blow.

Fifteen days later on March 6, Mac would fight Buddy Ryan at the Pyramid Club in Chicago to another draw. The descriptions of the match vary from the two going at it like *"game-cocks"* to it being scientific with very little in the ways of slugging. Again, depending on the source is what description you will get. What they all agree on is that in the six rounds the first three were even but Jack came out ahead in the fourth and fifth. The sources describe Ryan as a clever blocker but Jack as quick to take advantage of any mistake. During the fourth, Jack peppered Ryan with blows. In the sixth, Jack hit Ryan in the teeth, which led to him unleashing on *The Pride of Pittsburg,* winning the round. This was the last fight in Chi-Town of Jack's career.

Later, on March 28, a match between Kid Broad and Mac fell through. The bout was to take place at the Coliseum Club in Denver, Co. However, local politics got in the way. This turn of events transpired as Mac and Billy were on route and they did not find out until they arrived. The Fire and Police Board wanted to move the fight to the Denver Athletic Club, an amateur facility. This is what one source gave for the reason:

"The board has no objections to boxing contests under the auspice of the Denver Athletics [sic] Club, but draws the line against professionals fighting under professional conditions."

This means that they did not object to boxing if it is not in the professional capacity. The match fell apart and Mac and his manager waited out west to see what action they could cook up. One prospect was to take on the featherweight champion, Young Corbett II. Sadly, it never took place. Billy Corcoran and Mac waited for Young Corbett II to arrive in Denver to see if the two could box in a tent outside of the city. Corbett's manager turned down every proposition, even naming his own terms. This would not be the only time Corbett sidestepped Jack McClelland. Throughout the remainder of 1902, Billy or Red Mason (Mac's future manager and future manager of Harry "The Pittsburgh Windmill" Greb) would try to arrange a bout between Young Corbett II and Mac. However, the former would always turn down the offer.

On April 19, Mac was back in Toronto, Canada at the Mutual Street Ring to take on Billy Ryan. The six round bout met a premature end when the Deputy Chief of Police entered the ring during the third round, claiming both men fouled repeatedly and stopped the fight.

The papers speculated that the brutality of the bout was the cause of its termination. In the first round, Jack hit Ryan in the ribs and Ryan drew blood from Jacks nose. Jack hit him again in the ribs before the gong sounded and ended the round. In the second, Ryan hit Mac in the nose again and chased him around the ring. They came together, clinched, and Mac wrestled him to the floor. Upon getting up, Ryan landed two hits to Mac's face. At the opening of the third, the two fighters clinched and that is when the law stepped in and ended the fight. Even though it was a draw, the papers all agree that Ryan was the better of the two this match. Mac would return back home to begin training out on Perrysville Rd for his rematch against Ole Olson in June.

The "Chicago Swede" and the Irish boxer from the Hill would meet at the German Maennerchor Hall in McKees Rocks on June 2 in a six round bout. The match was originally scheduled for ten rounds but shortened to six and relabeled an exhibition with no decision to be given due to new boxing laws put on the books in Philadelphia and enforced by a local lawyer with the ironic name of John C. Haymaker.

The fans and papers would decide the outcome. Though Boxrec.com has it recorded as a win for Mac, it was actually a draw as neither knocked the other out. In front of 600 fans, the fight went the full six and then both fighters left the ring along with the ref.

That was how it ended. Reports in the papers say that Mac won the bout because he had Olson on the defense for most of the fight and in the sixth rained down blows to the face and body of the "Swede". However, because of the new laws, there was no decision. This was not just an isolated incident. The sport of boxing was constantly caught up in the revolving door of new laws and the evolving social mores of any particular year. This would be Jack's last fight until November.

On July 2, Jack would make it into the papers for another fight. However, this fight was during a political meeting in the Third Ward (The Hill) on July 1. The two Democrats, Boyle and Martin, wanted to control the room. Martin's side had control of the floor and would not relinquish to Boyle's party. In order to clear the room and give Boyle's people a chance to take the floor, Mac and boxer, Ed Dunn started fighting. By context of the article, it is clear that Mac was a Boyle supporter.

In August and September, Jack would referee two bouts. The first was on August 18 in Windber, PA between Davy Wayne & Denver Kid Davis. The second was at the Knoxville A.C. in the Allentown neighborhood of Pittsburg between Harry Brown and Tough Brogan. The month of October there is no mention of Jack in the sources. The last two months of 1902 would prove to be very busy for *The Pride of Pittsburg*.

On November 1, it was announced in the papers that Jack McClelland had split with Billy Corcoran and signed up with James "Red" Mason (to be known as Red Mason for the remainder of the text). Mason promising to do everything in his power to get Jack a title shot. His first bout under new management came on November 20 in Saint Louis at the West End club against Tommy Sullivan. This would be Jack's only win for the year. The bout was scheduled for fifteen rounds but lasted twelve when Mac delivered a blow to Sullivan's jaw sending him down to the mat. In another bizarre moment in McClelland's career, one of Sullivan's seconds ran alongside the ring and tried to revive his man with a splash of cold water to the face, an illegal move. The ref was too busy counting and holding Jack back with one hand to notice. Mac saw what was about to happen and ran over and punted the man in the face, sending him tumbling backwards over a chair. Just as the ref reached ten, Sullivan's other second threw in the towel. The fight was a big success. On November 24, the *Pittsburg Press* quoted H.W. Lanigan, a boxing writer as saying:

"The Wizard of Oz, or no other theatrical offering of the current season, ranks one-too-ten (sic) in points of spectacular features with the bout Jack McClelland and Tommy Sullivan put up at the West End Club last Thursday night."

At the same club on November 27, Jack would receive his first loss of the year against an unknown boxer from San Francisco named Eddie Toy. The twenty round fight ended in a decision in Toy's favor, which caused controversy. Reporters wiring the results to Pittsburg could not understand how the winner of the fight lay on the ground while the loser stood above him, under arrest along with his manager, until doctors could determine the outcome of Toy's injury or injuries. The papers state that Jack hit Toy with lefts and rights and that Toy could not keep up. In subsequent editions of the sporting sections of the local Pittsburg papers, there were articles claiming that referee Sharpe made the right call. The reports say that Toy held his own for the first nineteen rounds and that Jack only got lucky in the twentieth where he laid out Toy. In an ironic twist, Toy was trained by Abe Attell whom Jack would meet in 1904 in a controversial match that would become the highpoint of Mac's career.

In December 1902, Mac would fight three times. The first would be in Jackson, MI against Ole Olson on December 9. The fifteen round bout would be another draw. His next two fights would both end in draws but would cement Mac's name in the books as the only boxer at this time to fight one bout one day and then travel 600 miles to fight the next. His first match was against Hugh McPadden at the West End Athletic Club in St. Louis on December 18. One paper christened the Brooklyn boxer as *"the artful dodger"* for his ability to avoid McClelland. Just as Mac was about to take the lead, McPadden would go into the clinch.

There are even reports that McPadden fouled a few times but the fight continued. McPadden did open a wound over Mac's left eye that would play a role in his next fight on December 19.

At the conclusion of the bout with McPadden, Mason and Mac rushed 600 miles home to take on Eddie Toy in a rematch at Turner Hall, once located on Market St in the neighborhood of Manchester in Pittsburgh. During the ten rounds Toy went for the eye but Mac was able to avoid being beaten. As previously stated the fight ended in a draw thus concluding the 1902 fight year for *The Pride of Pittsburg.*

For the remainder of 1902, Mac would ref a match in Natrona and participate in a benefit for Frank McCloskey on New Year's Eve at Turner Hall, formerly located at the corner of Fifth and Marion in the Uptown section of Pittsburgh. As the year ended and festivities abound, Jack was only seventeen days away from his next fight.

Program from the Pittsburgh Cyclorama Company. Jack fought here on multiple occasions.

Courtesy of Historic Pittsburgh Full-Text Collection, Digital Research Library, University Library System, University of Pittsburgh..

Jack (left) and unknown boxer (right). The date and location of this photo are unknown.

Courtesy of Shirley Quaquarucci.

Cabinet Card of Jack McClelland. Taken at Sommer Studio in Philadelphia, Pennsylvania.

Courtesy of Shirley Quaquarucci.

The only known Jack McClelland autograph in existence.
Courtesy of Lisa McClelland & the estate of Dr. William D. McClelland.

From right to left: Dr. William D. McClelland, Jack McClelland, and Jack Dempsey. Date unknown.

Courtesy of Lisa McClelland & the estate of Dr.William D. McClelland.

Jack enjoying his retirement circa 1951.

Courtesy of Shirley Quaquarucci.

1903

While not the nadir year of boxing, 1903 was a low point for pugilists all around the nation. Prizefighting, already synonymous with violence and vice, was being driven from its former habitat by both the law and the church. As the reader will see, even former venues and neighborhoods that were friendly to the fight-game here in the *Smokey City* began to turn their backs on the Pugs that haunted their local sports sections and bar room conversations. One particular man, Attorney John C. Haymaker was a big player in this new movement.

In the book *Allegheny County, Pennsylvania; Illustrated* published in 1896, John C. Haymaker is described as a man of principle and the law. Admitted to the bar in 1875, he had a general law practice before entering the world of politics. In 1887, 1890 and 1893, he was elected Assistant Attorney General on the Republican ticket. After resigning his office in 1893, he ran for District Attorney and won in 1894. While it would be unfair to make him out to be a villain just for doing his job, he was part of the reason that boxing was on the decline in Pittsburg.

The reader can make up his or her own minds as to the magnitude his presence had on the tidal shift in Pittsburg boxing. Let us return to the main narrative and pick up with *The Pride of Pittsburg* as he is about to meet a former potter in the ring.

January 11, Jack is about to meet Crockey Boyle of Philadelphia at Arion Hall on Chartiers Street in Allegheny. Boyle was a former potter who started fighting four years prior to his bout with Mac. What made this new pugilist so special was that he took on the featherweight champion, Young Corbett II and won via points but did not gain the title. In fact, the sources state that he went toe-to-toe with the champion and never relied on the clinch. This was impressive to say the least and now Mac was going to take him on in front of a large crowd.

McClelland had Boyle worried from the start. The two met in the center of the ring at the beginning of round one and from that point on it was McClelland. However, Boyle did land some blows but by the seventh round, he was bleeding profusely and losing the match. In a last resort effort to win, Boyle resorted to the clinch.

This worked once and only once. Mac was ready for it the second time. The fight went the full ten and Mac won via points.

In the January 25 edition of the *Pittsburg Press,* Boyle was quick to blame a combination of factors on his loss to *The Pride of Pittsburg.* Everything from the lack of prep time, to the twelve-hour train ride stiffening up his body, to the incompetent refereeing of Jack Hannigan, worked in Jack's favor. Boyle wanted a rematch very badly but the two would never meet in the ring again.

In February, Red Mason went out to Philadelphia to try to arrange a fight between Corbett and Mac. This was unsuccessful as were all future attempts to fight Corbett. In fact, Mac would not have a crack at a champion until 1904. In the meantime, the shortest month of the year passed without Jack entering the ring. His next fight was against a record holder.

Andy Daley (sometimes misspelled as "Daly") was a former Boston boxer now fighting out of Chicago. Daley held a boxing record for fastest knockout. In six seconds, he sent Tom Duffy of Weburn (most likely a misspelling of Woburn), MA to the mat. The fight was originally supposed to take place on February 28 but due to a cold and orders from Jack's doctor, postponement was unavoidable.

By the time March 21 arrived both men were in perfect health and in perfect shape when they entered the ring at the National Athletic Club. The bout went the full ten rounds with Mac receiving a cut on the cheek and a cut above the right eye in the seventh round. In the final round, Mac chased Daley around the ring but as the latter went into a clinch and would not fight back. When the gong sounded, the match went to Mac but the decision had some fans and newspapers perplexed. The *Buffalo Enquirer* along with others said that the bout should have gone to Daley.

In April, Mac was back in Toronto, Canada in a rematch with Buddy Ryan. Sadly, no full write up of the bout exists today but a report from a week later says the fight was clearly a win for McClelland but the referee awarded it to Ryan. In fact, the one lone source states that the crowd was so angry at the decision that they chased the referee who escaped by climbing out a window.

In May, public opinion of the noble sport was starting to affect prizefighting in and around the city. The May 26 bout between

Mac and Billy Maynard of Philadelphia had to be cancelled due to overwhelming pressure from the residents of Millvale lead by Revered C.A. Boory. John C. Haymaker, the District Attorney, mentioned at the beginning of this chapter, stated that if any fighting were to take place at the Millvale Opera House both the combatants and the promoters were to be arrested on sight. This was enough to pull the plug and the fight never materialized anywhere else.

May 28, Jack was in Washington, Pa to fight Sam Meyers of New York. The sources state the crowd was small and the fight was uneventful. Red Mason refereed the match and Jack knocked down Meyers in the third round and ended the fight. What is strange about this is that the sources state that Myers got up after the ten count and he looked as fresh as he did at the beginning of the bout and went back to his corner with a smile on his face. No further explanation or speculation exists to clarify that report.

The months of June and July were uneventful save for a charity event at the Park Theater in Butler, PA. The show included boxing, wrestling, and vaudeville acts. Mac took on Ned Chernoff in an exhibition. With the coming of August came the chance to get back into the ring with Jack Hamilton. The fight was set to go on paper but the authorities in Kittanning, PA vetoed the proposition. This was the second time in 1903 that a fight ended before it even began for Jack McClelland.

Later that month on August 24, Mac was back in *Quaker City* to fight Sammy Smith. Philadelphia was ground zero for the new boxing laws that swept across the state like a wild fire and Jack's next two fights in the *City Of Brotherly Love* were under these constricting rules.

The six round bout at the National Athletic Club between Jack and Sammy Smith on the 24th went from a scientific match to chaos in three rounds. What exactly happened depends on what source you choose to believe. What they agree on is that in the third round Smith was ahead in points. Jack rushed at him and with a right to the jaw sent Smith into the ropes. Jack was now on top of Smith delivering blow after blow to his face. That is when one of Smith's seconds entered the ring and tried to either pull Jack off or throw him (again depending on the source). Jack kicked the man and at the same time, one of McClelland's seconds entered the ring and began fighting Smith's second. It did not take long for the police to enter into the equation and they broke up the two seconds. While all of this was going on the noise from the crowd drowned out the commands from the police for the two boxers to stop the match. They kept going and ended up in a clinch and depending on the source Jack used his head to butt Smith twice in the jaw or he did nothing at all. What they both agree on is that Smith kneed Jack in the groin at which point the police ended the fight with no decision.

One week later at the same venue, the two would meet again. This time their bout lasted six rounds with no decision. The papers and fans were unanimous in saying Mac won. However, there was no official decision under the new laws and so it is not counted amongst Jack's victories.

During his time out east there was a contest being set up in the west against "The Mexican" Aurelio Herrera for September 11. Portland, Oregon was the city and the venue was the Pastime Athletic Club. Jack and Mason went out there to begin training only to find out that the District Attorney, a man named Manning, had just recently abolished prizefighting and gambling in the city. As the reader can see, the attitude about prizefighting found in the earlier portion of this chapter was not confined to just Pennsylvania. Two other matches fell through, one being against African-American fighter "Rufe" Turner in Seattle. The authorities shut that match down before it even began.

Finally, a match in Tacoma, WA on October 21 got underway without interference from police or lawyers. The bout was against Tom Costello, a middleweight. The size difference did not matter as Mac knocked him out in the first round. At the sound of the gong, Costello hit Mac twice with a right and drew blood from his nose. Jack rushed Costello to the ropes, hit him with a right to the jaw and sent Costello to the ground. When he came to, he had a six inch cut along the back of his head where it encountered the edge of the stage.

Back home in November, Red Mason wrote an article for the *Pittsburg Press* describing the death of boxing across the nation. He goes on to explain that authorities are shutting down events in the west, which until just two months ago was a place where boxers and boxing were doing great and earning top dollar. Even San Francisco with its large arenas and its reputation as a boxing friendly town did not escape the tectonic shift, which shook the pugilist world. The reasons vary from it being a brutal sport, which could cause death or serious injury, to its attachment to the world of sin and vice. Public opinion and new social mores were sweeping the public mind and boxing was taking a hit.

The final month of the year found Jack involved in four different bouts. The first one took place on December 4 at the Badger Club in Milwaukie, WI. Charles Neary was undefeated in decisions but the fight ended with no decision being called as per the new state laws. Jack and Mason then returned to Pittsburg.

On December 8, Mason let the papers know his opinions on boxing in Pittsburg:

"The fighting game seems to be dead, or rather to have been killed in this vicinity. This cannot all be blamed on the authorities, for even when the sport was living in a healthy state there was always some to strike at its vitals by means of fake bouts."

Just a day before this quote John C. Haymaker shut down a ten round bout between Eddie Kennedy and Mull Bowser in Millvale. The reason behind this was a committee of forty lead by attorney E.C.Theobald who did not want prizefighting in their neighborhood. The Millvale Opera House, which was once the site of many boxing matches, was silent for the time being.

A new boxer on the scene, Jimmy Hanlon "The Fighting Marine" of Washington, PA challenged Jack to a fight in the papers. His name and challenge were almost daily appearances in the sports sections. The two would eventually meet up in 1904.

December 23, 24, and 25 were busy for McClelland. His next bout was at Turner Hall on Forbes St against George Engel. This was a boxing tournament with bouts going six rounds. Neither man could deliver the knockout blow and no decision could legally be called. Some of the sources state that Jack was the clear winner along with fans present at the match.

On Christmas Eve 1903, Jack was in Greensburg, PA in a charity-boxing event held at the Keaggy Theater. He took on Jimmy Reeder of Altoona in a six round bout.

Mac ended up braking his left hand in the first round but fought on until the end. Two doctors examined him and set the brake after the match. There was no decision.

His last fight was on Christmas Day. The sources state that Mac was going to fight in a private event against a well-known local boxer. The details are not forthcoming and even combing through Mac's personal notes no mention of this fight can be found. If it took place and against who and where will most likely remain a mystery.

As the reader can see, 1903 was a difficult year for those trying to earn a living in the sport of boxing. However, just like any other sport or trend, it would go through peaks-and-valleys up to and including today. This year might have been a low point for boxing in general but 1904 would see Jack at the pinnacle of his career in a match at the St. Louis World's Fair.

1904

Every athlete has that one season or year that defines his or her career. For Jack McClelland, that year was 1904. Though he would not know it yet, one upcoming fight would write his name into boxing history and become his legacy. As the calendar went from December 31 to January 1, Jack was just six months away from immortality.

With 1903 being a low point for boxing in the United States and for Jack, 1904 started out with talks of going across the pond to face some of the British Isles best fighters. Jack O'Brian was in talks with Mac and Mason to bring *The Pride of Pittsburg* to England. In the *Harrisburg Star-Independent*, O'Brian is quoted as saying:

"I can get McClelland a dozen and one matches and I feel sure he can win them. There is a fair class of small men in England, but the Americans are rather too skillful of them."

While a trip to England would have been great for Jack's career, it never materialized. His first fight of 1904 would be a little closer to home in Beaver Falls, PA.

At the close of 1903, Jimmy Hanlon, aka "The Fighting Marine", challenged Jack on an almost daily basis in the sports pages in various local papers. On January 14, he would get his chance to duke it out with McClelland in front of a six-hundred people for fifteen rounds under Marquis of Queensberry rules. In a lead up to the fight, Jack told the *Pittsburg Press*:

"I am going to win and I intend to waste no time upon it. I hope to secure a knockout. I know that Hanlon is a tough customer, for he has a good record, which I have carefully scanned. But I am not a bit afraid of the result. I am in the best possible physical condition, with the exception of my left hand, which I injured severely in my fight with Jimmy Reeder, at Greensburg. But the hand has been treated carefully, and I do not think it will go back on me. I will hold it back as much as possible and do the most punching with my right."

He also said:

"I am anxious to win this fight, for upon it depends several much better bouts. I have a chance to meet some of the best in the county, and that is the reason I want to make good tonight."

These words would turn out to be prophetic in nature within six months.

The fight was fast and over within four rounds. Jack had the upper hand from the sound of the first gong. He knocked down Hanlon three times in round one, twice in round two, with the gong saving him from a count out. In the third, he went down four times, each time from a right swing to the jaw. In the forth and final round he went down twice, with the final time being the end of the match. The final round went for one minute and forty seconds. Jack sent Hanlon, along with Byron McKeown (a wealthy oilman who was in attendance and betting on Hanlon) back to Washington County with a loss and lighter pockets.

Just two days later, *The Pride of Pittsburg* was back in *Quaker City* to fight Billy Willis at the National Athletic Club on January 16. While there is not much written about this match, the few sources all say that the bout went six rounds, with Jack as the clear winner, knocking Willis down ten times throughout the fight. There was no official decision awarded due to the laws governing boxing in Philadelphia. Boxingrec.com has the match listed as a loss for Jack but the sources and his personal notes list it as a win. Jack also reinjured his left hand during the bout.

The papers were a great place to brag about oneself and one's ability or to make a claim about holding a championship. In these early days of professional boxing, there was no shortage of people calling themselves the (insert weight class) champion. Jack was fighting in the featherweight division and his manager claimed in February that he was not only the state featherweight champion but also the true world featherweight champion, the qualifications for that being any boxer under 122. While the former may be an honorary title, the latter was very real and held by "The Little Hebrew" Abraham "Abe" Attell. Mason was convinced that his man could take Abe at any time. The two were just months away from meeting.

On January 28, at the Missouri Athletic Club in Kansas City, Mac was robbed of a win when he fought Kid Herman. The fight went twenty-rounds and Mac was clearly the winner but the referee, Dave Porter (or Porteous) ruled otherwise. In the *Pittsburg Press*, Mac said:

"Nearly everyone in the hall agreed that I had the best of the fight all the way. I could have put Herman out almost any time if I had wished to terminate the fight quickly. I was stronger at the finish than ever. I received very little punishment and this morning I feel as good as new. He could have never landed a blow had I not seen that it was easy, and allowed him to hit me, so that I could get close to him."

He later went on to say:

"However, the fight is over and I have nothing more to say. But I challenge Herman to 10 or 20 rounds-or let it go to 50 for all I care-to be fought anywhere but Kansas City. I will concede anything except Kansas City. That man Porteous must not be the referee. He is a thief pure and simple. Had any other man been officiating last night, the decision would have been mine. I certainly earned it, but was robbed. I agree to fight Herman at any time –let him give me one week's time to get in training, and I will punch his head off. If I fail to put him out inside of 20 rounds, I will give him my share of the receipts. That is how confident I am of beating him."

The *Pittsburg Gazette* states that Herman knocked down Mac in both the first and tenth rounds but Jack was the more scientific of the two men. He just could not deliver the knockout blow. On the other hand, Herman was hitting hard but not doing much damage. One eyewitness claimed that the referee fled the building after announcing the decision. This may be true as Mason stated he was holding McClelland back from attacking Porter. The exact reasons why it went to a draw are unclear and no further information is available giving the referees side of the story.

February was a quiet month for Jack save for a three round exhibition match with Kid Tyler at Old City Hall on the 13th for a boxing and vaudeville show. At this time, he was still working out and preparing himself for any challenges that lay ahead. His name was still in the papers on a regular basis but not always for the best of reasons. In an article written by Red Mason, Mac's manager, he stated that while Jack has been making good money for over eight years in the fight game, he has nothing saved for his retirement. The exact reason(s) why Jack was broke are unknown and no information is available in the historic record or in family history to shed light on his financial problemsm, save for rumors of alcoholism.

On March 16, a bout between Mac and Jerome Haney at Rexbury Park (most likely a misspelling of Roxbury Park) in Johnstown, PA was cancelled due to threats of arrest at the hands of Sheriff Samuel L Lenhart by orders of the District Attorney and Judge F.J. O'Conner. As the reader has seen in the previous chapter, the attitudes towards professional prizefighting and professional boxers were changing from a socially acceptable pastime and career to that of a sport that damaged the public and glorified violence and vice. Later that month on the 28th, Jack would have a rematch with Jack Hamilton in Beaver Falls. The fight went the full fifteen rounds with Mac winning via points. One point of interest is that Mac was fighting at 128, well above his usual ringside weight.

On April 6, the long awaited bout between Mac and Tim Callahan finally materialized. Over the years the two had matches scheduled that ended before they began for a variety of reasons too numerous to list. The South Sharon Athletic Club would host the event at the Broadway Opera House. By all descriptions the fight was lackluster, some even thought it was fake (the exact reasons why are unclear). The bout ended in a draw after ten rounds. Boxingrec.com has the fight listed as a win for Mac but this is at odds with the primary sources.

A chance accident by Benny Yanger in May changed the course of Jack's career and legacy forever. Yanger was scheduled to fight Kid Goodman at the West End Athletic Club in St. Louis, MO on May 12 but hurt his hand playing ball. Mac stepped in and began getting into shape at the Business Mens Gymnasium located at 806 & 808 Fifth Ave in Pittsburg. He would run until lunchtime and workout after lunch, sometimes in front of an audience. His trip to St. Louis and subsequent two fights would play out against the backdrop of a global event held that year in *Mound City*, the 1904 World's Fair.

The *Louisiana Purchase Exposition*, also known as the St. Louis World's Fair ran from April 30-December 1, 1904. Just like previous World's Fairs, such as the 1893 *Columbian Exposition* and the *Exposition Universelle* held in Paris during the year 1900,

St. Louis became the focal point and travel destination for tens-of-thousands of people from around the globe seeking adventure and entertainment. This was the place to be to be during 1904, especially for those looking to make a name for themselves. Jack and Mason decided to make St. Louis their home for the next few weeks.

May 12 came and Jack found himself in less than perfect shape against Kid Goodman, a tough opponent. However, he fought well and the ten-round bout went to a draw. Both sides were satisfied with the outcome and Jack went into training for his next opponent on June 2, whoever that may be.

Rumors began to circulate in the papers about a possible match between *The Pride of Pittsburg* and "The Little Hebrew". Jack was in full training mode. This was the opportunity of a lifetime. He was never able to schedule a fight with Young Corbett II when he was the featherweight champion but now it looked as if a chance at a championship was at hand. When it was finally announced, Mac was not only about to enter the squared circle, but into the pages of boxing history.

Abraham Washington "Abe" Attell was a fighter from San Francisco. In an age where ethnic backgrounds played into the fighters persona, being Jewish made him stand out amongst the Irish and African-American fighters of the time. Attell won the vacated world featherweight championship after defeating Johnny Reagan. Afterwards, Attell became a larger-than-life figure in the boxing world. The fight between Jack and Abe would be one that haunted *The Pride of Pittsburg* until his dying days.

On June 2, at the West End Athletic Club, Jack McClelland entered the ring to take on the World Champion. Odds were in favor of Attell at 10-4. Attell's reputation and record were the reason for this. The Saint Louis Dispatch stated, *"Abe will punish Jack"* and there was good reason to believe so with his fighting ability. This was going to be the fight of Mac's life.

Abe entered the ring at 122, while Jack refused to weigh in stating that the fighters agreed on catch weight, though Mason said, he could not have been over 128. This little piece of information would become a point of contention when the fight was over. At the sound of the gong, the fifteen round bout began under Marquis of Queensberry rules.

The following account of the fight comes from many different sources and from personal notes and interviews given by Jack in his later years. When in question, the author chose to use the most neutral and common account of the fight and steered clear from those with a bias, though those do exist out there in the sources and newspapers.

During the opening of the fight, Attell was in the lead but not by much. In the third round, he landed a huge hit that stunned Mac, but as one paper put it, *"he came back strong as an ox"*. In addition, by the end of the third round the momentum of the fight began to shift in Mac's favor. From the end of the third through the tenth round, Mac was able to hold Abe at bay with punches, blocks, and dodges. Everything was going McClelland's way; Abe was slowing down while he was speeding up. It was clear by the thirteenth round that the champion did not stand a chance against the *Smokey City* fighter. What happened next was one of the most unusual events in the early history of professional boxing. In order to get a clear picture of what happened we need to go back to round twelve.

At the start of the twelfth round, Abe was going for the long headshots while Mac was looking for body blows. Abe went into the clinch more often than he did before the 10th. He was unable to avoid Mac's rushes. At one point in the round Abe went into the clinch but was careless and Mac got in three or four hits to the stomach. The ref cautioned the two about low blows. This call may be the reason why Attell claimed a foul in thirteenth.

Mac targeted the blow that caused the controversy as one writer from the *St Louis Dispatch* said *"between the false ribs & the groin"*. Attell pushed Mac's hand lower and then claimed a foul. He fell to the floor and writhed in pain. Abe returned to his corner to recuperate for two or three minutes, depending on the source. This was unusual as it violated the Marquis of Queensberry rule of ten seconds. The decision by referee Sharpe (or Sharp) to allow stoppage of the fight is controversial to this day. The following is from the *St. Louis Republic* regarding the rules;

"The ninth clause of the Marquis of Queensberry rules provides that the referee shall decide questions not provided for in the rules themselves in case of an emergency. But the fifth clause provides that if a contestant is knocked down, he must arise within ten seconds or be considered defeated. And the seventh and eighth clauses provides that if a foul, which the referee deemed deliberate or likely to injure the chances of a contestant be committed, the offender shall be disqualified."

All of these factors came into play in the decision by Sharpe to stop the fight. This did not sit well with the fans who stormed the ring. Men began to argue with their neighbor about the validity of the call. A riot was about to erupt. Sharpe decided that if Abe wanted a decision by foul he would have to submit to a medical exam by a doctor. "The Little Hebrew" declined and went back out to fight. As this was going on, Jack was standing in a state of limbo waiting to either fight or be declared champion. When Abe came out, he danced around the ring like a man who did not sustain an injury to the sensitive groin area. The *Saint Louis Republic* commented as much on this in their write up of the fight.

At the sound of the gong in the fifteenth round, in front of four-thousand people, Jack McClelland had defeated the Worlds Featherweight Champion by decision via points. However, the title would not change hands. Due to Jack's refusal to weigh in at the beginning of the fight and the title being limited to men under 122; Jack was too heavy to be a featherweight champion. This point did not sit well with Mac as he said the fighters agreed on catch weight with nothing said about being under 122.

Eyewitness to the fight such as former Australian pugilist, Jimmy Ryan said the blow that send Attell to the ground was murderous but fair. Tom Corbett, brother of the famous boxer, James J Corbett, said the blow was six inches too high to be a foul. It was unanimous throughout the sporting pages in every major city that Jack was the clear winner and that Attell played a dirty trick in order to avoid losing via knockout.

Red Mason and Jack McClelland did not go quietly into the night but made their opinions known in many publications about their feelings towards Abe and the fight itself. In the *Pittsburg Press*, Mason had this to say:

"All I have to say is I always said McClelland was a champion, and to-night proves it. McClelland won by a knockout in the thirteenth round, but just to show he could win I sent him for the next two rounds and won again after Attell had a five minutes rest."

Mac had this to say:

"I had him going all the way after the tenth round, and I really had him out in the thirteenth when I pasted him in the body with both hands in quick succession. He went down like a log, but his friends claimed a foul. They said I had hit him below the belt. I did nothing of the sort, and despite the fact that Sharpe was Attell's own choice of a referee, he was fair enough to see that I was fighting fairly and that I had committed no foul. That blow settled Attell but on the account of the squabble he was allowed to come back into the ring."

"However, I am well satisfied to have received the decision on points, although I had him most decisively beaten all the way."

Years later in 1948, the *Pittsburgh Sun-Telegraph* ran a

two-day story on "Pittsburgh's Forgotten Fighter". In an interview conducted with the now seventy-five year old, *The Pride of Pittsburg* recalls saying,

"What's the matter, Abe, do you want to quit?" as Abe lay on the ground. When later asked if Attell was the greatest opponent he ever faced, Jack replied, *"I can't say that because I never liked him."*

The McClelland-Attell bout would be the apex of Jack's career. Even though he did not walk away with the championship, he is remembered today as the conqueror of Abe Attell. However, this was not the end of Mac's career.

On June 22, the papers stated that Mac had to go back East to take care of his son who sustained an injury while playing.

"The boy is 8 years old now and is a lively little chap. He is always playing in the streets and I don't know what happened to him. I kept the wires hot asking for information, but could get no response."

At this time in his life, Mac was married to a woman named Rose. The couple had two children, John and Charlie. Which son and the exact nature of the injury is not clear but he did head home at the request of his progeny. Mac left the 1904 World's Fair for good.

On July 4, Mac was in Bay City, Michigan in a ten round exhibition with Young Kid McCoy. A no knockout rule was in place and Jack was warned that if he tried he would be arrested on the spot. The papers all agree that Mac had the better of the bout.

As the summer wound down, Mac was back in Philly on August 12 to take on George Decker at the National Athletic Club. The same "no decision rule" was still in effect so the fighters had to win via knockout. The six round bout ended with no winner decided but the papers state that Jack sent Decker down to the canvas several times, once with a series of lefts and rights to the jaw in the second round. Besides the second and sixth round, the fight had very little action.

On September 19, Jack took on New Castle pug, Jimmy Dunn at the Broadway Opera House in South Sharon, PA. Both fighters weighed in at 127. The twelve round bout was uneven and in favor of *The Pride of Pittsburg*. Mac had the advantage from the start of round one. He hit Dunn at will and very rarely took blows. Dunn went into the clinch for the majority of the fight to save himself. At one point during the seventh round, he clung to Jack's legs, trying to save himself from a knockdown. Jack toyed with him for the remainder of the bout. At the end of the twelfth round, Mac was the clear winner but there was no decision awarded.

Sometimes two fighters can draw such a big audience that the previously booked venue turns out to be inadequate to accommodate the crowd size. The McClelland-Stroup bout is a perfect example. The match was originally supposed to take place at the Coyle Theater in Charleroi, PA but had to be moved at the last minute to the Gamble Opera House in Monongahela. This worked out great for fans coming in via streetcar. Monongahela was thirty-five minutes closer to the city. This fight scheduled for October 17 would go fifteen rounds and have a winner. While no play-by-play of the fight exists in any of the sources, they all agree that Jack was the winner via points in the final round. The papers also report that Stroup was bleeding badly by the end of the fight. This would be the last professional match for Jack in 1904.

On November 3, there was a match scheduled against Benny Yanger but he backed out at the last minute for reasons unknown. Jack then went into training for a bout in December against Loudon Campbell, a friend and teacher.

As the reader may recall Campbell and Mac came up together during the latter years of the nineteenth century with Cambell teaching Jack how to use his left. The venue for the fight was the Business Mens Gymnasium, the same place Jack trained. It would be a six round bout, hosted by the Herron Hill Athletic Club. The bout was part of a boxing card that evening for a smoker (a professional prize-fight conducted under the auspices of a private, charitable club in those jurisdictions which prohibited prize-fighting, but allow amature bouts). The Boxingrec.com site states that Jack fought Charlie Atkinson, but this is incorrect. Atkinson took on another boxer that evening. December 23 was the night of the smoker and also the night when the police began to really crackdown on prizefighting in the city.

The preliminary bouts went on without a hitch but as soon as Jack and Loudon entered the ring, Inspector Robinson, under orders of Director of Public Safety Moore, put a stop to it before it began. The police were now enforcing the edict that no professional fighters can box within the city at clubs or smokers. Director Moore had this to say to the *Pittsburg Press*:

"Boxing Promoters must understand that we mean exactly what we say when we refuse to allow professionals in boxing in Pittsburg. I do not think that it is necessary to add anything to what was printed in the Press last week concerning the attitudes of the Public Safety Department. I had given no specific orders to Inspector Robinson to stop the bout last night between Campbell and McClelland. The police department was acting in accord with the general orders issued some time ago."

While the crowd was not happy with this mandate, there was no disorder in its wake. Mac fought Paul Moore instead in a friendly three (or four depending on the source) round bout. Campbell took on another man as well. Thus, the two would not meet in the ring this time. They would not step into the ring again together until 1917.

As the year ended, the career of Jack McClelland would begin its downward trajectory. The once bright star of the *Smokey City* would begin to fade out just as the year faded into history.

The following year would not be remembered for excellence in the ring but trouble with the law.

1905

When one delves into historic research to mine for facts, sometimes that answer is less than forthcoming. On occasion there is no answer to be found for a variety of reasons too numerous to list. However, sometimes there is more than one answer and it makes it just as difficult to ascertain the reality of what really happened. Case in point, the failed matchup between Mac and Reeder on January 7, 1905.

The month of January can be unforgiving in Pennsylvania, especially in the western half of the state. Lake-Effect Snow and polar winds can shut down businesses, schools, highways, and all but emergency services within a matter of hours. In the case of a boxing match in Johnstown against Jimmy Reeder, people took heed of the inclement weather and did not attend thus forcing the management to call off the bout. Well, that is what one paper says happened.

Another paper says that Jimmy Reeder and his manager, who were the owners of The Brownstone Athletic Club, got into an argument and Reeder left town. Another says that the owner refused to open the doors because there was no assurance of being paid. While the final paper says that Jack's manager, Red Mason told him to skip the fight and concentrate on his next match against Solly Stroup. Whatever the reason, the two did not fight and we will never know for sure which one of these, if any, was the real reason for the contests termination.

One week later, Jack was a no-show for a fight against Solly Stroup in Altoona, PA. One paper states that Jack was sick and could not box. Others say he just did not show up and called him unreliable. Again, there is no one alive today that can give us the real story of why Jack was not there. What we do know for sure is what happened the next night in Pittsburg.

On January 15, 1905 William T. McClelland, older brother and backer of Jack was not elected alderman of the second district of Pittsburg. He lost to Emil Sparr, who won by a large margin. This did not sit well with the McClelland faction. They marched down to the where the votes were tallied and demanded to see the numbers. What happened next does not make a lot of sense.

When the McClelland's arrived, an African-American man by the name of Abe Hall took the tally totals and swallowed them.

What is even more bizarre is that Hall was a McClelland supporter. Regrettably, this action would unleash the fury of Jack McClelland and his brother Charlie on Hall. They beat him at the corner of Centre Ave and Soho St and then went into William T. McClelland's pool hall where supporters began recasting their ballots. McClelland did not become alderman but the altercation with Hall would come back to haunt Jack and Charlie later in the year.

The next time we find Jack in the historical record is on March 18 where he is set to fight Young Kid McCoy at Coliseum Hall in McKeesport. The bout was part of a larger card held as a smoker for the Olympia Club. Police officers would not interfere with the six round exhibition as the coordinators of the smoker received a permit from Police Chief L.E. Rotzsch. There is no play-by-play of this rematch between the two. However, word spread that Jack's performance was lackluster and that McCoy won the bout. Mason responded in the papers that this was untrue and Mac would be happy to have a rematch with the man any day.

April brought another man from Jack's past back into the ring for a rematch, the fearsome fighter, Kid Broad from Cleveland. The papers were abuzz with news pouring in daily that articles were signed, clubs were bidding on the match, and that "sports" from all over the area were ready to see the bout of the year. The date was set for April 26 and the Nonpareil Club in Beaver Falls would be the venue. Broad came into town early and even refereed a six round exhibition between Al Martin of Warren, PA and McClelland at the Gamble Opera House in Monongahela. The match went by fast with lots of clinching happening in the first two rounds. Jack also kept Martin busy dodging his rights. In the fourth, Martin landed one on Jack's nose, which sent *The Pride of Pittsburg* into a frenzy of body blows. In the fifth, Martin swung and missed Jack, who in turn hit him in the stomach with a devastating blow. The sixth was an even round with both fighters looking just as fresh as they did in the first. Broad later commented that if he were to have given a decision it would have gone to Mac.

On the 20th, Mac was back in Johnstown at the Cambria Theater to fight Kid Carter. Again, there is no play-by-play in the historic record but the *Pittsburg Press* comments that Jack showed "*superior form and generalship*". The bout was a draw.

April 26 arrived and people poured out of the city and onto the trains heading for Beaver Falls for the epic fifteen-round bout. When they arrived, they would bear witness to one of the most bizarre stories in Pittsburgh boxing history. In short, Broad would not fight. The house had only collected $400. He said that he fought for much larger sums and the purse was just too small. He wanted a cut of the receipts from the gate but the club would not accommodate him. Broad stayed backstage and refused to enter the ring. His manager went out and explained to the audience the reasons why Broad refused to fight and that if a collection were taken up maybe they could convince him to enter the ring. A hat went around and $100 was netted from fight fans. Broad said that he would go out now, but only for ten rounds. Red Mason said that Mac only fights fifteen or nothing at all. At this point an hour past the official start time had elapsed. Another hour later, after going back and forth, Mason finally convinced Kid Broad to fight the full fifteen. Then another problem arose. While all of this was going on, Jack retreated to his hotel room and went to bed. When Mason finally found him, Jack said he would not get up for $1000. That ended any chance of people seeing the fight between Kid Broad and Jack McClelland. Three-hundred fans left disappointed and one paper claims, without a refund (while another says the club did reimburse the people). Sadly, the winner would have gone on to fight Young Corbett II but that would be impossible now. May would pass without any news but June brought on three episodes of legal trouble for *The Pride of Pittsburg* starting on June 5 in Monongahela, PA.

Red Mason had a stable of fighters, one being Mac. Another was Larry Temple, an African-African fighter. Temple was going to fight George Cole at the Gamble Opera House with Mac as one of Temple's seconds. There would also be two other preliminary fights, one with another of Mason's men, Young Zerringer who fought Patsy Brannigan. This would be the only fight that got underway that evening. What happened next put an end to the festivities. Harris, the referee, called the fight a draw. Mason jumped into the ring and told the ref that his man clearly won.

Mason then knocked Harris down with a sharp blow to the face. The chief of police, Leo Logan, a former boxer and glass blower jumped in the ring and knocked out Mason. Then Jack got involved and tried to save his manger. He took a swing at Logan with a left, but the former boxer dodged and knocked Mac out. Later, he and a doorman named Harry Mellon (or Mullen) were taken to jail. Mellon was charged with interfering with a police office (how and/or why is unknown) and Mac was charged with assault and battery, along with resisting arrest. Both spent the night in jail with a hearing scheduled for June 6.

While this was going on Mason, who came to, fled the scene with Temple and Cole. The trio left Monongahela by foot and went to the next town over, New Eagle where they were spotted later that night. It is most likely they took a trolly back into Pittsburg from there, avoiding the police in Monongahela who would be looking for them.

The next day, a Finleyville man named John B. Hays bailed out Jack to the sum of $500. Jack had met Hays on his way to the fight the night before. It is unclear if this was a gift or if the man expected repayment. Jack then went back to Pittsburg where his legal troubles were just beginning.

By this time in their marriage, Rose and Jack were not together. There are family stories about alcohol and women but the former cannot be confirmed with concrete historic documentation. The latter though does have some truth. Jack had another son to another woman named Klemenski, who according to Shirley Quaquarucci may have been a hat maker. Their son's name was Lee and he would go on to become a mail carrier. Jack would later live with Lee's family at the end of his life. Regardless of unhappiness, infidelity, or alcohol, Jack had two other sons, John and Charles whom he owed support. On June 12, Rose was in Criminal Court with a constable asking that Mac fall in line with the court order to give the family $4 a week. According to one source she had Jack arrested in 1904 for non-payment but no record survives to verify this claim (if indeed it was true). By June, Mac was $52 dollars behind in support and the judge advised Rose to file an attachment against Jack's bondholder, Red Mason. This would not be the last of this in 1905 nor in the years to come.

"This is a case in which the jury has paid absolutely no attention to the evidence."

These words came from Judge John M Kennedy on June 22 when the jury of twelve found Jack and his brother Charlie "not guilty" of assault and battery against Abe Hall. Hall took the McClelland's to court stating that Mac and Charlie attacked him at the corner of Centre Ave and Soho St during the election in January. He told the jury that Mac hit him with brass knuckles and then pointed a gun at his head before hitting him with a club. The McClelland's admitted to assaulting Hall but only after Hall hit their aged father. They also stated that Jack used no weapons of any kind but his fists. One could chalk up the jury's decision to the attitudes of people towards African-Americans in the early twenty century or maybe the McClelland's story was true after all. Sadly, there are no living eyewitnesses today to give us the real story. What happened that January day will always remain a mystery.

In July, Mac was in West Alexandria, PA with Larry Temple training for a bout in Bridgeport, OH (just across the river from

Wheeling, WV). His opponent would be Jimmy Dunn. In a lead up to the July 31 bout Mac had this to say in the *Pittsburg Post*:

"Dunn is a promising boxer, but I have not the least doubt that he will be easy money."

The day of the fight arrived and in front of one-thousand one-hundred people, the match went to a draw. The papers reported that Mac took a defensive position instead of his usual offensive one. The two would go into clinches with Dunn using his left to get out of them. The papers also reported that the crowd was not happy with the way Mac used his head in the clinch or his elbows to get out. There were no knockdowns or injuries during the six rounds.

Sadly, August 11 would be Mac's last match of the year. He was up against the man he was supposed to fight in January, Jimmy Reeder. The bout took place in Altoona and went six rounds with no decision, though the sources say that Mac was the better of the two. The papers also state that Reeder was a bloody mess by the end of the last round. He went down to the canvas a total of seven times and the last time got up on the nine count. Each time he would get to his feet, Mac would send him right back down. Mason later said in an article that the ref would not stop the fight even though another punch could have killed Reeder.

On September 29, Mason was arrested and taken to court on charges of fraud. He was the bondsman for Jack (known as J.A. McClelland in the article) and he was now responsible for the payments Jack owed Rose. Mason was on the hook for up to $300. The problem was that Mason had not been truthful about his assets, which included property he claimed to own that was worth $3,000. When they tried to collect money from Mason, he had none. He did not even own the property he claimed. Thus, when he signed on as Jack's bondsman he was lying to the court about his worth. This event most likely led to the parting of ways between Mac and Mason.

On October 1, Mason announced in the papers that he was no longer booking fights for or looking after Jack McClelland. Mason claimed that Jack's health was the reason and that nine years of boxing had taken its toll on the pugilist from the Hill District. It is hard not to see the connection between the arrest and this move but then one has to abandon the realm of concrete historic fact and enter into the lands of speculation. Later, on October 8, Mason was back in court and he swore that he did not intend to commit fraud when he signed on as Jack's bondsman.

The rest of the year was very rocky for *The Pride of Pittsburg*. On November 17, Jack did not show up at a scheduled fight with Jimmy Hanlon "The Fighting Marine" in Connellsville, Pa. No explanation or reason exists as to why he was a no-show. In December, Jack once again in trouble with the law.

On December 11, 1905, there was a scheduled fight between *The Pride of Pittsburg* and "Syracuse" Billy Ryan in Monongahela. The bout was part of a charity event to help the widows and orphans of the Hazel Kirk Mine Disaster. While this fight did not take place that day (the event was moved to January of 1906 and the opponent would be Kid Carter), Jack was involved in another altercation that evening instead.

While on a streetcar on Wylie Ave, Jack attacked a black man for not giving up his seat for a white woman. Again, we find two different versions with different details in two different papers. The following is a combination of both.

A man named Charlie Turner (or George W. Davis) was riding the streetcar with Jack. In one account, the man had a boy on his knee. When a white woman got onboard, Jack told Turner (Davis) to get up. The man either did not stand or just moved over to make room. The man's action (or lack thereof) angered Jack and he said:

"Get up, or I will spit in your eye and break your face."

Jack then gave the man an uppercut sending his head through the plate glass window behind him. This caused a panic and Officer Lenkner arrested both men. Jack was fined either $1 or $25 with both in agreeance that the other man was let go. This was not one of the prouder moments in the career of Jack McClelland. Even the papers were beginning to comment on his behavior. The *Pittsburg Press* had this to say:

"Jack McClelland is sure keeping in the limelight, but not in his former way."

The last few days of the year found Jack in Monongahela, PA training for an upcoming bout with Kid Carter in January. The glory days of *The Pride of Pittsburg* were well behind him now.

Over the next few years, there would be few fights but multiple run-ins with the law.

1906-1909

During the early part of the twentieth century, mine disasters were an all too common occurrences in the United States. In Southwestern Pennsylvania, the Hazel Kirk Mine Disaster was one of many in this coal rich region. However, that did not mean it was any less traumatic for those left behind. The communities of these victims would ban together to try and help the women and children left without financial support due to a sudden and tragic loss of life. Fundraisers were common and a variety of benefit shows took place to give some financial stability to the families affected. With the Hazel Kirk Mine Disaster, the city of Monongahela held a benefit show featuring boxing at the Opera House where Jack McClelland would take on Kid Carter for six-rounds on January 3, 1906.

There was some controversy about holding a boxing benefit show in the city. Local churchgoers and a minister planned to protest the event but eventually relented as long as there was no referee in the ring and no decision rendered. While this worked at first, during the McClosky-Rowe bout, the action became so brutal that the local authorities were going to shut down the show. A compromise came when they allowed a man to enter the ring to make sure that the clinches were broken and the rough work curtailed, as long as he did not have the title of "referee". By the time of the main event, things were back in order.

In front of nine-hundred fans, *The Pride of Pittsburg* came out strong during the first three rounds. However, during the fourth Carter began to rush Jack around the ring. From this point until the end of the sixth, it was all Kid Carter. At the end of the bout, Jack was groggy and spent. While there was no official decision, it was clear to the fans and the press that Kid Carter won the bout. Sadly, this would be only one of two fights *The Pride of Pittsburg* would have during the year 1906. From this fight until September, Jacks only opponent was the law.

On April 15, Jack McClelland, along with his brother Charlie, found himself sitting in the Centre Ave police station along with either nine or twelve other men (depending on the source). The McClelland brothers were running an illegal gambling house on La Place Street, just off Centre Ave in the Hill District. One paper names the facility as the *Jack McClelland Club* while the other does not. It is unclear if this was a bar or a private home where illegal activity was taking place. The police raided the facility along with other locations around the city (those others did not belonging to the McClelland's), in an attempt to crack down on gambling and other unlawful doings. What came of this arrest is unknown. The author cannot locate any documentation at the time of writing that would fill in the missing details. However, the McClelland's were back in the Hill District in September of 1906 to participate in one of the most bizarre stories ever associated with boxing outside of Sonny Liston.

Shortly before seven o'clock on Sunday September 5, a riot broke out at the corner of Centre Ave and Soho St in the Hill District. Between one-to-two thousand people, either fought in or witnessed the Irish-Americans and the African-American hitting each other with fists, bricks, and clubs, all over a pocket watch. It had started earlier that day when Larry Gibson accused John Keefer of stealing his pocket watch. The three McClelland brothers were there as well (William, Charlie, and Jack). However, the accusation went unresolved. Later that night Gibson and Keefer went back at it again, this time outside the club owned by William T. McClelland at the corner mentioned above. As the two began to fight, Officer Charlie Allen, an African-American, tried to arrest both Gibson and Keefer. William did not like the way the officer was handling the prisoners and got involved. This is where the details get muddy and contradictory depending on the source, but at some point Officer Allen calls in Constable H.P Barclay and Eugene Philips (both African-Americans) to assist in the arrest and to help keep order. The events that follow seems to be lifted straight from a Scorsese film.

The three McClelland brothers, along with the father William Sr, head down the road to their home at 2318 Centre Ave and retrieve two (or three, depending on the source) hand guns and start back to the scene of the altercation. Allen and Barclay not only see them coming back, they also see the weapons. A shoot out was about to happen on Centre Ave. Barclay and Allen took out their guns in anticipation of what is to come. While all of this is going on, whites and blacks from the all over the neighborhood came down to the corner of Centre and Soho and a race riot soon broke out. Both sides unleashing their hatred of the other. Meanwhile the McClelland's and the authorities were about to have a showdown.

While there is no record of who fired the first shot, what is known is that twenty shots were fired in total. Three of the bullets came from the gun of H.P Barclay and found their target, William T. McClelland Jr. He took two shots to the leg and sustained a nasty injury to the scalp from a bullet grazing his head. It is unknown how many, if any, shots Jack fired.

Eventually the Pittsburg police from both the Centre Ave Station and Oakland ended the riot. With a heavy use of mace and horse drawn police patrol wagons, the rioters scattered to the winds fearing arrest. All-and-all only nine arrests were made that day. Three of them were the McClelland brothers. Willaim was rushed to Passavant Hospital to have his wounds treated while Charlie and Jack were taken the police station.

On the morning of the seventh, Jack and Charlie posted one-thousand dollars bail and waved a hearing before Magistrate F. J

Bradly at the Centre Ave Police Station. This was not the end of the story for the McClelland's and their involvement in the riot.

Just ten days later on the seventeenth, a lawsuit was filed against Jack and his brother, William (the current holder of Jack's bond) to collect the five-hundred dollars that was owed to Rose McClelland for back spousal support. This would come back to haunt Jack later.

On September 28 (boxingrec.com has the incorrect date of the 23rd), we find Jack in the ring for the last time in 1906. This time he is up against Al Weaver of Warren, PA at Irwindale Park in a ten-round bout. Unfortunately, there is no blow-by-blow description of the fight in any of the sources. The only detail forthcoming is that the fight was a draw.

October would hold more legal trouble for Jack McClelland. Prothonotary William B Kicker issued a capias (a writ ordering the arrest of an individual) for failure to pay back spousal support to Rose McClelland. What made this case unique was that Judge Samuel A McClung of the Court of Common Pleas 3 made it legal for the first time for a prothonotary to issue a capias in a wife desertion case, thus making legal history.

Jack would make one more appearance in the papers in 1906 with a challenge to all 126-130 fighters, especially in the New Castle and Erie area.

All is quiet until January of 1907 when a fight between Mac and Joe Bernstein was scheduled for the eleventh. This fight did not take places for reasons unknown.

On February 13, Mac enters the ring for the first time since September to take on Al Martin in Greensburg, PA for the Greensburg Athletic Club. The Master of Ceremonies and referee that evening was none other than Red Mason, Jack's former manager. Both the papers and Mason said he was in good fighting form. The men fought six rounds to no decision but everyone was impressed with Jacks performance. This would be Jack's only match in the year 1907. Legal troubles were on the horizon.

On February 18, 1907, the trial began to prosecute the McClelland brothers for their involvement in the riot the previous

September. The charges at the time were felonious assault and battery with the intent to kill. By the time the jury reached a verdict, the charges for Jack and Charlie were dropped to aggravated assault and battery. This carried a lighter sentence while William faced felonious assault and battery, a more serious crime. In the end, Jack and Charlie received a ten-dollar fine each and sixty days in the workhouse. William's fine was in the amount of one-hundred dollars and a one-year stay at the workhouse. This would be the last entry for Jack in 1907 save for a mention by Red Mason that he saw Jack training at the gym in December.

On February 6, 1908, Jack entered the ring for the first time in almost a year to take on Jimmie "Skip" Manning. The six-round exhibition took place at the Hatfield Outing Club on Butler St in Lawrenceville. While there was no winner, the exhibition demonstrated that Jack was not out of the fight game just yet.

For three months, Jack had been in training at the Hatfield Outing Club for his upcoming match with Kid Tyler. The veteran boxer was in great shape and ready to take on a much younger man. The venue for this bout was May's Hall in Ambridge, PA, just off the Fort Wayne Railroad line. The bout took place on February 12, 1908 with between five-hundred to a thousand in attendance (depending on the source). However, all the papers agree that Kid Tyler won the bout, even though it was ruled a draw. While the papers do agree Tyler was the clear winner, the details differ from source to source. The following paragraph is a brief summary of how the fight went.

The *Post* said Jack was in fine shape and that if he could pull off a victory there was some interest from Philadelphia in bringing him out East. At the sound of the gong, Tyler rushed Mac and got a right to his face. Mac returned the favor with a right/left to the head. They went into a clinch and Tyler landed some blows on Mac before the round was over. This pretty much sums up how the fight went. Tyler would rush Mac and hit him while *The Pride of Pittsburg* would retaliate with a few blows. It was clear that Tyler was in much better shape and a better boxer at this time than Mac. During the fifth round, Tyler sent Mac to the floor. The referee began the count. At three, Tyler went over and helped Jack back up and the gong sounded. At the end of the fight, Tyler looked fresh and ready to go another ten while Jacks back was bruised from all the punches he sustained while both in the clinch and in the break, (they fought under straight rules, which allowed for hitting while tied up or breaking the clinch). William McClelland was not happy with the ruling and thought his man had won. He made a scene and entered the ring to argue with the referee, who later had a hard time getting out of the hall in fear of William McClelland attacking him.

One final bout that month was scheduled for February 21 in Parkersburg, WV against Kid Hemlick but the swollen river made this impossible due to the venues location near the riverbank. The next time Jack was in the papers was not for a fight but for abandonment and desertion.

The *Gazette-Times* reported in the March 21 issue that sheriffs going to the home of Mrs. Jack McClelland, located in the Knoxville section of Pittsburg, to serve eviction papers found an awful scene. When the sheriffs knocked, the door opened and the oldest child stood there. He immediately began to beg the men for food, as did his younger brother. When the men entered, they found an infant in rags lying on the floor. There was no furniture or heat inside. The mother, Mrs. Jack McClelland was ill and in bed. Half crazed she admitted to trying to kill herself because she could not take care of the four children in the home. The men removed the family from the premises and took them to the jail. Later, the children were sent to Marshalsea (later called Mayview Hospital). This was a home for orphans and abandon children as well as the insane. Mrs. Jack McClelland threatened to kill herself again when she heard her children were being taken from her. What became of these four children is unknown. The identity of Mrs. Jack McClelland is unknown as well. He had only two children to Rose (John and Charlie) and another son, Lee to a woman named Klemenski. What makes this even more complicated is that Jack was still legally married to Rose. Therefore, if he was married to both he was a bigamist. Upon reaching out to some relatives of Jack's, the author learned that the two youngest children in this home were Jack's, not the two oldest and that Jack was married to two different women at the same time. However, this cannot be verified with primary sources. Further questioning revealed that they had no idea what happened to the children taken to Marshalsea. This will have to remain a mystery for now.

Jack's last fight in 1908 would be against Ned "The Fighting Hebrew" Chernoff in Monessen, PA. The ten-round fight was at catch weight but only went six-rounds before the referee called the bout a draw. Neither man wanted to engage the other so they just moved around the ring. The audience began to boo and hiss. Chernoff landed a few hits but by all accounts, the fight was tame.

In August, Jack was brought before the court on charges of desertion and failure to pay support to his wife Rose. Judge Swearingen allowed Jack to be released without bail following a plea from his attorney. This was just the beginning of Jack's legal troubles that year.

On October 10, 1908, Jack is sent to jail for failure to pay spousal support to Rose. His lawyer, Edward G. Coll pleaded with Judge Frazer to give him one more chance. However, Judge Frazer did not grant Jack that opportunity. Jack swore that he tried to get a job at the filtration plant and at the Pittsburg Railway Company but was unsuccessful. Judge Frazer was not buying it and said he doubted very much that McClelland even went looking for work. He also pointed out that Jack's wife, Rose, found work making a dollar a night scrubbing floors and that she was more successful than he was. Judge Frazer told Jack he could go free if he could pay the bond owed, however, he could not. Thus, Jack went to the Allegheny County Jail under Warden Edward Lewis for the remainder of 1908.

On January 17, 1909, Judge Marshall Brown freed Jack from jail. He promised to start paying the four dollars a week owned to Rose. Jack's lawyer, Edward G. Coll told the judge that Jack was in demand in the ring and that the money would help to pay support. This was partially true.

In the beginning months on 1909, Jack ran the Fifth Ward Club out of Belmont Hall (his brother's property and the site of the pool hall). He booked matches like the February 2 bout between Patsy Brannigan and Young Fitzgerald of Milwaukee as well as acted as referee. He also refereed matches outside of the Fifth Ward Club at Old City Hall, Beaver Falls, and at Miller Hall in East Pittsburg. The bout at Miller Hall on April 12 was supposed to be Tommy Lynch verses Reddy Moore. However, attendance was so low that Moore decided not to fight. Jack boxed a six-round exhibition against Lynch for the crowd instead. The last mention of Jack was in April when he refereed a bout at the Sterling Club. This was the last time he made the news in 1909. In the following two years, Jack would try to make a comeback. He would start training and fighting again on a somewhat regular basis. What follows were the *Comeback Years*.

1910-1911

If 1900 was the *Year of the Rematch* and 1902 was the *Year of the Draw* then the years 1910 & 1911 should be called the *Comeback Years*. Jack McClelland was coming out of a three-year self-destructive tailspin. He was set to make a comeback and reclaim his rightful title, *The Pride of Pittsburg*. However, as far back as March 12, 1906 the *Gazette-Times* led off an article with a not-so-subtle assessment of Mac:

"Jack McClelland who used to be the Pride of Pittsburgh in his palmy days..."

In the late summer of 1910, just as the heat began to diminish and the season ended, Jack McClelland was preparing to make his comeback into the world of professional boxing. The *Smokey City* pugilist was out in New Bethlehem, PA for over a month training his body and putting on shows, all in an effort to reclaim his place among the best fighters in the world. His comeback match was just around the corner.

On September 18 at Kelly Ring in Homewood, Jack McClelland entered the squared circle for the first time since 1908. It is impossible to say what he was thinking or feeling, but the papers wrote that he looked great. He was back to his old fighting weight at 122. Across the ring was George Blackwell, a pugilist from Wilkinsburg. The stage was set for Mac to make his comeback and he did not disappoint.

It was a cock-eyed fight right from the start. Blackwell only landed one punch the entire match. During the first round, he hit Jack in the heart but that did not stop *The Pride of Pittsburg* from sticking his left glove in Blackwell's face while dancing around the bewildered boxer, who was swinging at the air. This was going to be a very difficult six-round match for George Blackwell.

The papers claim that the referee should have stopped the fight in the third. Jack hit him with a devastating right that sent him spinning out of control to the floor. The ref began to count. Blackwell got back up but went right back down to the canvas. He got back up and went into the clinch to save himself. For the reminder of the bout it was all Mac. The papers commented that one could see the shadow of his former self, as he looked just as fresh in the sixth as he did in the first. This was the first win for

Mac and a great way to begin his comeback. However, his luck would soon change just a month later.

On October 3, Jack entered the ring at Old City Hall to take on Leo McAuliffe, a tough North Side fighter. This time the fight did not go as planned. The sources all agree that Jack won the first round. One paper even states that he went back to his corner, with a cocky smile as if the match was already in the bag. That was a huge mistake.

In the second, Leo hit Mac with a hard left swing to the jaw and sent him to the mat. Mac got up and went into the clinch. In the third, Mac was able to avoid danger by ducking, dodging, and going into the clinch once again to stave off a defeat. In the fourth, Mac was cornered and Leo hit him with a stiff left to the left eye, almost closing it and reopening an old scar that bled freely. In the fifth, Mac had his left glove in the face of Leo and jabbed away to no avail. In the sixth, Leo rushed Jack around the ring. He put Mac down to the mat with a left. Mac got back up and landed a few light punches but it was obviously over for *The Pride of Pittsburg*. At the sound of the gong, it was clear that McAuliffe was the winner. Though defeated, the audience cheered for the veteran fighter as he left the ring. Even his old rival, Yock Henniger gave him praise in the papers the next day.

Just a few days later on Oct 15, Mac was back at Old City Hall to take on Cliff Ford of Chicago. Though the fight was scheduled for six-rounds, it lasted four with Jack coming out on top via a K.O. Described as a *"classy opponent"* by the papers, Cliff never got over a left to the face in the first round. Jack had him going at every turn. He knocked Ford down in the third but he got up just before the fatal ten was uttered. He was not so lucky in the fourth when he took a right punch and rolled repeatedly on the canvas. By the time he got back up, it was well past ten seconds. Disgusted, he went back to his corner, not before growling at the referee.

November was a busy month for *The Pride of Pittsburg*. On Nov 5, he knocked Dick "Kid" McCoy through the ropes in the fourth at Old City Hall to claim yet another victory. Just fourteen days later on the 20th he and Hank "Kiddus" McCloskey performed boxing stunts to warm up the audience before the Trendell-Britt fight at Old City Hall. What these "stunts" were is unknown. Just as the month was about to close, Jack was back in the ring again to take on a young fighter from Greenfield.

Jeddy McFadden came to Old City Hall on November 26 with many fans from the neighborhood. In fact, a large section of seats were bought and reserved just for them. The fight went six-rounds and ended in a draw according to Boxingrec.com. The papers say that while McFadden did most of the work, Mac had the best punches, including a right to the jaw in the second. Who exactly won is a bit of a mystery. Two papers claim Mac outpointed McFadden and gave him the win, while another says it is a draw. Boxingrec.com has it listed as a draw as well. As there is no one decision we will never know for sure.

In the last month of the year, Jack was part of a benefit for newspaperman, Bill Dwyer, at the Southside Market Building on the 13th. His opponent was Jerome Hanley. While no play-by-play exists, the papers say Jack beat Hanley with ease. However, his luck was about to run out again in a rematch with Jeddy McFadden on December 17.

Back at Old City Hall, McFadden came this time to take down the veteran boxer. The fight did not even last six rounds. During the second McFadden hit Jack in the chin and sent him to the floor. While the hit was not powerful enough to knock out *The Pride of Pittsburg,* his head bouncing off the ground was. In fact, he was dragged back to his corner by his seconds and it took a minute to revive him.

The year 1911 dawned and Jack lay low for the first two months. He reentered the ring on March 25 against Johnny McCleary (or Creeley or Greely, no one source has the same name) at Old City Hall. The Brooklyn boxer took Mac's left jabs and kept coming back for more. Jack looked visibly winded but came out on top via points at the end of six-rounds.

The last fight of Jack's career was a rematch against George Blackwell, the same man whom he took on at the beginning of his comeback. At the Hiland Theater in the East End of Pittsburg on April 18, Jack McClelland lost to the younger man. It was evident that Jack's glory days were behind him. Blackwell pummeled him from the second to the sixth and did not let up. Jack went to the canvas many times that match. In the end, he went the distance for six-rounds but lost out via points.

It is fitting that Mac's last mention in the papers in 1911 has him as a referee at the open-air arena in Kennywood Park on September 4, Labor Day. Labor Day was and is the last day when the park is open. The participants and the outcome of the bout are unimportant. However, one can only imagine the sun setting over the park, the warm glow of summer coming to an end and with it, the career of Jack McClelland, aka *The Pride of Pittsburg*.

1912-1954

Though Jack's career ended in 1911, he was still in the boxing game on-and-off for about five years. During the years 1912 and 1913, he was refereeing matches in-and-around the Pittsburgh area. This kept his name in the sports section. However, one starts to notice that writers bring up his name more in a historical context than contemporary. He becomes a living relic of a bygone era. These articles range from speculation about his lack of a title to Jack's own words about his career. Two questions seem to be the cornerstones of these pieces, "*Why wasn't he the champion*" and "*What went wrong with his comeback*". There are many theories and rumors of the former but one writer, Guy Richard, states that Mac could have been champion; however, his carelessness in the ring and lax training habits prevented him from making it to the top.

Mac had his own ideas on the latter subject about his "comeback". In an article, published in 1914 he admits that he was slowing down and did not have the speed he once had. He says that if his opponent fought slowly he could take them, however once they sped up he could not compete. The sport is a young man's game and he was past his prime.

By the year 1915, Jack had moved onto a different career. Loudon Campbell employed him in his automobile business as a chauffeur. In a somewhat comical piece from 1915, the readers of the local papers find Jack broken down on Liberty Ave, unable to get his car started. He is perspiring and fuming, trying to get the vehicle back up and running. It was not until former outfielder, Buck Sweeny (whose entire career consisted of playing one inning in one game for the Philadelphia Athletic in 1914) comes along and helps Jack get back on the road by helping crank the car.

Over the next two years, articles state that he is a mechanic for Campbell instead of a chauffeur. The reason for the change is unclear. What is clear though is these two pugilists came up together in the 90's but never once fought in the ring professionally. The reason why was due to a weight dispute. Mac wanted to fight at 122 while Campbell wanted 126-130. They could never come together on this. The reader will remember they were scheduled to box at a smoker but the authorities shut it down, thus they never found out who was the better fighter. This would change in the year 1917 when the two put on a boxing exhibition at Turner Hall in Lawrenceville for the family of the late Billy McIsaac. There was no winner but they put on one great show for the fans. This would be the last time Mac would ever enter a boxing ring in gloves.

In 1918, Mac is working for the city in a garage on Wylie Ave in the Hill. Ironically, the building that housed the city automobiles was the same one he worked in as a postilion boy thirty years prior as a youth. He worked there at least until 1930; however, his exact year of retirement from the position of mechanic is unknown at the time of writing. Around this time, his name begins to vanish from the pages of the newspapers as well, even in the historic context. There are some brief mentions during the latter 1930's. In 1938 his brother and backer, William passed away from complications of diabetes. In 1939, the papers report Jack is critically ill in his North Side home. The nature of this illness is unknown.

The author had the chance to interview his last living relative that knew him personally, Mrs. Shirley Quaquarucci in November of 2017. The information obtained painted a picture a man who was enjoying the golden years of his life. He was not much for television but listened to music or the Pirate games on the radio. He did not attend many fights and declined most offers. There is a picture of Mac and Jack Dempsey along with Mac's nephew, Dr. William D. McClelland but the date of the photo is unknown. His granddaughter, Shirley remembers his love of veal cutlets, and his hobby of sitting with a neighbor across the street from his house on a homemade bench, chewing Waymens brand tobacco and gossiping about the neighbors. The only other habit he had was going to bed early. He lived with his son, Lee (born 1904) and Lee's wife and children on Rothpletz St up until his death in 1954.

On November 19, Jack fought his last battle, this time for his life. The cause of death was a Cerebral Vascular Accident that occurred a few days prior. He was taken to Woodville Hospital but died none-the-less. He was 82 years old. His funeral took place at Novak's Funeral Home on Brighton Rd and his body interred at Highwood Cemetery in section 7 plot 939.

What is there left to say about a man who some consider one of the greatest boxers Pittsburgh has ever produced? His career started at the end of the bare knuckles era and before the greats like Billy Conn. He fought in opera houses, barns, clubhouses, and on barges anchored in the river. He fought in a time where the laws pertaining to boxing shifted like the winds. He beat a champion but never gained the title. His career influenced others that gained more popularity while he faded into obscurity. The public may have forgotten Jack McClelland today but his memory lives on with boxing historians and on the internet with folks like Douglas Cavanaugh of *Pittsburgh Boxing: A Pictorial History* on Facebook. The author hopes this book will renew interest in a man who symbolizes the hard work and dedication that has made this city great. In the end, the author's greatest hope is that this forgotten fighter is remembered once again alongside all the other greats and he takes his place once more as *The Pride of Pittsburg.*

Bibliography

1873-1895

1. Gruber, John H. "The Fighters of Pittsburg: A Series of Articles About Boxers Who Made Ring History in Western Pennsylvania During Bygone Years. XIII Jack M'Clelland". *Pittsburgh Daily Post* (Pittsburgh, PA), Feb. 03, 1918.
2. Rooney, Dan, and Carol Peterson. *Allegheny City*. Pittsburgh: University of Pittsburgh Press, 2013.
3. Unknown. *The Battle of Gettysburg: As exhibited by the Pittsburgh Cyclorama Company*. Pittsburgh: Shaw Brothers Printers, 1890. http://historicpittsburgh.org/islandora/object/pitt%3A31735056290392
4. Jab, Jim. "Woman Won Wager When She Snuck into Boxing Show". *The Pittsburg Press* (Pittsburgh, PA), Dec. 12, 1911.
5. Jab, Jim. "Fistic Foibles". *The Pittsburg Press* (Pittsburg, PA), Aug. 05, 1910.
6. Keck, Harry. "Jack McClelland Pittsburgh's Forgotten Fighter". *Pittsburgh Sun-Telegraph* (Pittsburgh, PA), Feb. 17, 1948.
7. Keck, Harry. "Jack McClelland Pittsburgh's Forgotten Fighter". *Pittsburgh Sun-Telegraph* (Pittsburgh, PA), Feb. 18, 1948.
8. Beers, Paul B. *"Pennsylvania Politics Today and Yesterday"*. Philadelphia: A Keystone Book, 1980.

1896

1. Gruber, John H. "The Fighters of Pittsburg: A Series of Articles About Boxers Who Made Ring History in Western Pennsylvania During Bygone Years. XIII Jack M'Clelland". *Pittsburgh Daily Post* (Pittsburgh, PA), Feb. 03, 1918.
2. Unknown. "Today May Settle Matters". *The Wheeling Daily Intelligencer* (Wheeling, WV), Feb. 29, 1896.
3. Jab, Jim. "Ring Remembrances". *The Pittsburgh Press* (Pittsburgh, PA) Jan. 28, 1918.
4. Unknown. "Sporting in General". *The Pittsburg Press* (Pittsburg, PA), Jan. 13, 1896.
5. Unknown. "Deed I'se Can't Mr. Buck". *The Philadelphia Inquirer* (Philadelphia, PA), Dec. 2, 1898.
6. Unknown.. "McClelland Covers Smiths Money". *Pittsburg Daily Post* (Pittsburg, PA), Oct. 10 1896.
7. Unknown. "McClelland Means Business". *Pittsburg Daily Post* (Pittsburg, PA), Oct. 4, 1896.
8. Unknown. "Sporting Notes". *Pittsburg Post* (Pittsburg, PA) Oct. 17, 1896.
9. Unknown. "Pugilistic Pointers". *The Pittsburg Press*. (Pittsburg, PA) Oct. 20, 1896.
10. Unknown. "M'Clelland Wins". *The Pittsburg Post* (Pittsburg, PA) Nov. 17, 1896.
11. Unknown: "Jack McClelland wins on a foul from Chicagoan." *The Inter Ocean (*Chicago, IL) Nov.17, 1896.
12. Unknown. "Sporting Notes". *The Pittsburg Post* (Pittsburg, PA) Nov.18, 1896.
13. Unknown. "A Large Entry List". *The Pittsburg Press* (Pittsburg, PA) Nov.15 1896.
14. Unknown. "Pugilistic Pointers". *The Pittsburg Press* (Pittsburg, PA) Nov.20.1896.
15. Unknown. "McClelland & McGrath". *The Pittsburg Post* (Pittsburgh, PA) Nov. 25, 1896.
16. Unknown. "Pugilistic Pointers". *The Pittsburg Press* (Pittsburg, PA) Nov. 25, 1896.
17. Unknown. "Boxers Have their Innings". *The Pittsburg Post* (Pittsburg, PA) Nov. 30, 1896.
18. Unknown. "McClelland and Smith". *The Pittsburg Post* (Pittsburg, PA) Dec. 06, 1896.
19. Unknown. "Pugilistic Pointers". *The Pittsburg Post* (Pittsburg, PA) Dec. 10, 1896.
20. Unknown. "Fun in the Gymnasium". *The Pittsburg Commercial Gazette* (Pittsburg, PA) Dec. 15, 1896.
21. Unknown. "Bedford A.C Entertainment". *The Pittsburg Post* (Pittsburg, PA) Dec.22, 1896.

1897

1. Gruber, John H. *"The Fighters of Pittsburg: A Series of Articles About Boxers Who Made Ring History in Western Pennsylvania During Bygone Years. XIII Jack M'Clelland"*. Pittsburgh Daily Post (Pittsburgh, PA), Feb. 03, 1918.
2. Unknown. "Pugilistic Pointers". *The Pittsburg Post* (Pittsburg, PA) Jan. 23, 1897.
3. Unknown. "McGrath's Blood Poisoned". *The Pittsburg Post* (Pittsburg, PA) Jan. 23, 1897.
4. Unknown. "Live Sporting Notes". *Chicago Tribune Review* (Chicago, IL) Feb. 08, 1897.
5. Unknown. "McGrath & McClelland". *The Pittsburg Post* (Pittsburg, PA) Feb. 09, 1897.
6. Unknown. "McGrath & McClelland". *The Pittsburg Post* (Pittsburg, PA) Feb. 11, 1897.
7. Unknown. "Prize Fight". *The Daily News* (Salem, OH) Feb. 12, 1897.
8. Unknown. "McClelland Gets The Purse". *The Pittsburg Post* (Pittsburg, PA) Feb. 12, 1897.
9. Unknown. "Five Events Pulled off At Braddock: Some Boxers Missing". *The Pittsburg Post* (Pittsburg, PA) Feb. 26, 1897.
10. Unknown. "Won in Three Rounds". *The Pittsburg Press* (Pittsburg, PA) Mar. 17, 1897.
11. Unknown. "McClelland in Three Rounds". *The Pittsburg Post* (Pittsburg, PA) Mar. 17, 1897.
12. Unknown. "Sporting Notes". *The Pittsburg Post* (Pittsburg, PA) Mar. 18, 1897.
13. Unknown. "Pugilist Pointers". *The Pittsburg Press* (Pittsburg, PA) Mar. 31, 1897.
14. Unknown. "McClelland Defeats Leopold". *The Pittsburg Post* (Pittsburg, PA) Mar. 31, 1897.
15. Unknown. "McClelland and Murphy". *The Pittsburg Post* (Pittsburg, PA) Apr. 02, 1897.
16. Unknown. "No Match Made". *The Pittsburg Post* (Pittsburg, PA) Apr. 04, 1897.
17. Unknown. "Among the Boxers". *The Pittsburg Post* (Pittsburg, PA) Apr. 06, 1897.
18. Unknown. "Among the Boxers". *The Pittsburg Post* (Pittsburg, PA) Apr. 18, 1897.
19. Unknown. "Pugilistic Pointers". *The Pittsburg Post* (Pittsburg, PA) Apr. 21, 1897.
20. Unknown. "Another for McClelland". *The Pittsburg Post* (Pittsburg, PA) Apr. 22, 1897.
21. Unknown. "Murphy Knocked Out". *The Pittsburg Press* (Pittsburg, PA) Apr. 22, 1897.
22. Unknown. "Among the Boxers". *The Pittsburg Post* (Pittsburg, PA) Apr. 26, 1897.

23. Unknown. "Among the Boxers". *The Pittsburg Post* (Pittsburg, PA) May. 03, 1897.
24. Unknown. "Among the Boxers". *The Pittsburg Post* (Pittsburg, PA) June. 04, 1897.
25. Unknown. "Pugilistic Pointers". *The Pittsburg Press* (Pittsburg, PA) June. 04, 1897.
26. Unknown. "Among the Boxers". *The Pittsburg Post* (Pittsburg, PA) July. 01, 1897.
27. Unknown. "Among the Boxers". *The Pittsburg Post* (Pittsburg, PA) Aug. 28, 1897.
28. Bernard Postal, Jesse Silver, and Roy Silver. *Encyclopedia of JEWS in sports*. New York: Bloch Publishing Co, 1965.
29. Unknown. "Among the Boxers". *The Pittsburg Post* (Pittsburg, PA) Oct. 27, 1897.
30. Unknown. "Among the Boxers". *The Pittsburg Post* (Pittsburg, PA) Oct. 31, 1897.
31. Unknown. "Among the Boxers". *The Pittsburg Post* (Pittsburg, PA) Nov. 09, 1897.
32. Unknown. "Pugilistic Pointers". *The Pittsburg Press* (Pittsburg, PA) Nov. 13, 1897.
33. Unknown. "Among the Boxers". *The Pittsburg Post* (Pittsburg, PA) Nov. 23, 1897.
34. Unknown. "Among the Boxers". *The Pittsburg Post* (Pittsburg, PA) Nov. 27, 1897.
35. Unknown. "Among the Boxers". *The Pittsburg Post* (Pittsburg, PA) Dec. 01, 1897.
36. Unknown. "Among the Boxers". *The Pittsburg Post* (Pittsburg, PA) Dec. 07, 1897.
37. Unknown. "Among the Boxers". *The Pittsburg Post* (Pittsburg, PA) Dec. 08, 1897.
38. Unknown. "Ready for a Fright". *The Pittsburg Post* (Pittsburg, PA) Dec. 09, 1897.
39. Unknown. "McClelland's Easy Fight". *The Pittsburg Press* (Pittsburg, PA) Dec. 10, 1897.
40. Unknown. "Among the Boxers". *The Pittsburg Post* (Pittsburg, PA) Dec. 10, 1897.
41. Unknown. "Kinlow and McClelland". *The Pittsburg Post* (Pittsburg, PA) Dec. 12, 1897.
42. Unknown. "Pugilistic Pointers". *The Pittsburg Press* (Pittsburg, PA) Dec. 14, 1897.
43. Unknown. "Pugilistic Pointers". *The Pittsburg Press* (Pittsburg, PA) Dec. 16, 1897.
44. Unknown. "Among the Boxers". *The Pittsburg Press* (Pittsburg, PA) Dec. 19, 1897.

1898

1. Gruber, John H. "The Fighters of Pittsburg: A Series of Articles About Boxers Who Made Ring History in Western Pennsylvania During Bygone Years. XIII Jack M'Clelland". *Pittsburgh Daily Post* (Pittsburgh, PA), Feb. 03, 1918.
2. Unknown. "St. Paul Kid". *The Saint Paul Globe* (Saint Paul, MN) Jan. 14, 1898.
3. Unknown. "Among the Boxers". *The Pittsburg Post* (Pittsburg, PA) Jan. 15, 1898.
4. Unknown. "Among the Boxers". *The Pittsburg Post* (Pittsburg, PA) Jan. 22, 1898.
5. Unknown. "Among the Boxers". *The Pittsburg Post* (Pittsburg, PA) Feb. 01, 1898.
6. Unknown. "Among the Boxers". *The Pittsburg Post* (Pittsburg, PA) Feb. 21, 1898.
7. Unknown. "Among the Boxers". *The Pittsburg Post* (Pittsburg, PA) Feb. 26, 1898.
8. Unknown. "Another Draw". *The Pittsburg Press* (Pittsburg, PA) Mar. 01, 1898.
9. Unknown. "Among the Boxers". *The Pittsburg Post* (Pittsburg, PA) Mat. 10, 1898.
10. Unknown. "Yock Henniger and Jack M'Clelland". *The Pittsburg Post* (Pittsburg, PA) Mar 13, 1898.
11. Unknown, "All Sorts". *The Enquirer* (Cincinnati, OH) Apr 10, 1898.
12. Macon, "Gossip About The Boxers". *The Enquirer* (Cincinnati, OH) Apr 17, 1898.
13. Ralston, Guy L. "Believe it or Not". *The Pittsburgh Gazette-Times* (Pittsburgh, PA) Aug 6, 1922.
14. Hutchison, David C. *Boxing*. New York: Outing Publishing Company, 1913.
15. Keck, Harry "Sports". *The Pittsburgh Sun-Telegraph* (Pittsburgh. PA) Nov.25, 1954.
16. Keck, Harry "Keck Says:" *The Pittsburgh Sun-Telegraph* (Pittsburgh. PA) Date unknown.
17. Unknown. "Among the Boxers". *The Pittsburg Post* (Pittsburg, PA) Mar. 16, 1898.
18. Unknown. "Among the Boxers". *The Pittsburg Post* (Pittsburg, PA) Mar. 28, 1898.
19. Unknown. "Among the Boxers". *The Pittsburg Post* (Pittsburg, PA) Mar. 29, 1898.
20. Unknown. "Pugilistic Pointers". *The Pittsburg Press* (Pittsburg, PA) Mar. 31, 1898.
21. Unknown. "Among the Boxers". *The Pittsburg Post* (Pittsburg, PA) Apr. 02, 1898.
22. Unknown. "Boxers Little Boxers Big". *The Pittsburg Post* (Pittsburg, PA) Apr. 03, 1898.

23. Unknown. "M'Clelland Wins in Nineteen Rounds". *The Pittsburg Post* (Pittsburg, PA) Apr. 05 1898.
24. Unknown. "Among the Boxers". *The Pittsburg Post* (Pittsburg, PA) Apr. 06, 1898.
25. Unknown. "Boxers Little Boxers Big". *The Pittsburg Post* (Pittsburg, PA) Apr. 24, 1898.
26. Unknown. "M'Clelland Defeats Kinlow". *The Pittsburg Post* (Pittsburg, PA) Apr. 26, 1898.
27. Unknown. "Among the Boxers". *The Pittsburg Post* (Pittsburg, PA) May. 04, 1898.
28. Unknown. "Among the Boxers". *The Pittsburg Post* (Pittsburg, PA) May. 15, 1898.
29. Unknown. "Boxers Little Boxers Big". *The Pittsburg Post* (Pittsburg, PA) May. 22, 1898.
30. Unknown. "Among the Boxers". *The Pittsburg Post* (Pittsburg, PA) May. 29, 1898.
31. Unknown. "Among the Boxers". *The Pittsburg Post* (Pittsburg, PA) June. 03, 1898.
32. Unknown. "M'Clelland and Gardner". *The Pittsburg Post* (Pittsburg, PA) June. 08, 1898.
33. Unknown. "Boxing". *The Wheeling Intelligencer* (Wheeling, WV) June. 08, 1898.
34. Unknown. "Pugilistic Pointers". *The Pittsburg Press* (Pittsburg, PA) June. 09, 1898.
35. Unknown. "Among the Boxers". *The Pittsburg Post* (Pittsburg, PA) June. 09, 1898.
36. Unknown. "Another for Gardner". *The Wheeling Intelligencer* (Wheeling, WV) July. 01, 1898.
37. Unknown. "Among the Boxers". *The Pittsburg Post* (Pittsburg, PA) Sep. 15, 1898.
38. Unknown. "Pugilistic Pointers". *The Pittsburg Press* (Pittsburg, PA) Nov. 10, 1898.
39. Unknown. "Among the Boxers". *The Pittsburg Post* (Pittsburg, PA) Nov. 11, 1898.
40. Unknown. "Among the Boxers". *The Pittsburg Post* (Pittsburg, PA) Nov. 13, 1898.
41. Unknown. "Pugilistic Pointers". *The Pittsburg Press* (Pittsburg, PA) Nov. 16, 1898.
42. Unknown. "Among the Boxers". *The Pittsburg Post* (Pittsburg, PA) Nov. 22, 1898.
43. Unknown. "Among the Boxers". *The Pittsburg Post* (Pittsburg, PA) Nov. 26, 1898.
44. Unknown. "Boxers Little Boxers Big". *The Pittsburg Post* (Pittsburg, PA) Dec. 04, 1898.
45. Unknown. "Among the Boxers". *The Pittsburg Post* (Pittsburg, PA) Dec. 05, 1898.

46. Unknown. "Bout Ended In A Draw". *The Pittsburg Post* (Pittsburg, PA) Dec. 06, 1898.
47. Unknown. "Among the Boxers". *The Pittsburg Post* (Pittsburg, PA) Dec. 07, 1898.
48. Unknown. "No boxing in Homestead". *The Pittsburg Post* (Pittsburg, PA) Dec. 16, 1898.
49. Unknown. "Boxers Little Boxers Big". *The Pittsburg Post* (Pittsburg, PA) Dec. 25, 1898.
50. Unknown. "Fistic Encounters in the Local Ring". *The Pittsburg Post* (Pittsburg, PA) Dec. 29, 1898.
51. Unknown. "Among the Boxers". *The Pittsburg Post* (Pittsburg, PA) Dec. 30, 1898.
52. Unknown. "Among the Boxers". *The Pittsburg Post* (Pittsburg, PA) Dec. 31, 1898.

1899

1. Gruber, John H. "The Fighters of Pittsburg: A Series of Articles About Boxers Who Made Ring History in Western Pennsylvania During Bygone Years. XIII Jack M'Clelland". *Pittsburgh Daily Post* (Pittsburgh, PA), Feb. 03, 1918.
2. Unknown. "Stevens May Object". *The Pittsburg Press* (Pittsburg, PA) Jan. 01, 1899.
3. Unknown. "Pugilistic Pointers". *The Pittsburg Press* (Pittsburg, PA) Jan. 12, 1899.
4. Unknown. "Pugilistic Pointers". *The Pittsburg Press* (Pittsburg, PA) Jan. 14, 1899.
5. Unknown. "Pugilistic Pointers". *The Pittsburg Press* (Pittsburg, PA) Jan. 23, 1899.
6. Unknown. "Hogan and McClelland". *The Pittsburg Press* (Pittsburg, PA) Jan. 25, 1899.
7. Unknown. "Among the Pugs". *The Pittsburg Press* (Pittsburg, PA) Feb. 03, 1899.
8. Unknown. "Hogan and M'Clelland". *The Pittsburg Press* (Pittsburg, PA) Feb. 05, 1899.
9. Unknown. "Among the Pugs". *The Pittsburg Press* (Pittsburg, PA) Feb. 08, 1899.
10. Unknown. "Among the Pugs". *The Pittsburg Press* (Pittsburg, PA) Feb. 10, 1899.
11. Unknown. "Twenty Round Draw". *The Pittsburg Commercial Gazette* (Pittsburg, PA) Feb. 14, 1899.
12. Unknown. "Sporting News". *The Pittsburg Press* (Pittsburg, PA) Feb. 17, 1899.
13. Unknown. "Very Fast Fight". *The Pittsburg Commercial Gazette* (Pittsburg, PA) Feb. 25, 1899.
14. Unknown. "Among the Pugs". *The Pittsburg Press* (Pittsburg, PA) Mar. 26, 1899.
15. Unknown. "All the Sporting News". *The Pittsburg Press* (Pittsburg, PA) Apr. 08, 1899.
16. Unknown. "All the Sporting News". *The Pittsburg Press* (Pittsburg, PA) Apr. 10, 1899.
17. Unknown. "Jack M'Clelland: Pride of Pittsburg". *The Pittsburg Post* (Pittsburg, PA) Apr. 16, 1899.
18. Unknown. "Among the Pugs". *The Pittsburg Press* (Pittsburg, PA) Apr. 18, 1899.
19. Unknown. "Among the Pugs". *The Pittsburg Press* (Pittsburg, PA) May. 02, 1899.
20. Unknown. "Gardner in Distress". *The Pittsburg Press* (Pittsburg, PA) May. 02, 1899.
21. Unknown. "Jack M'Clelland in Twenty Rounds". *The Pittsburg Post* (Pittsburg, PA) May. 02, 1899.

22. Unknown. "To Save His Brother". *The Pittsburg Commercial Gazette* (Pittsburg, PA) May. 02, 1899.
23. Unknown. "Among the Boxers". *The Pittsburg Post* (Pittsburg, PA) May. 03, 1899.
24. Unknown. "Among the Boxers". *The Pittsburg Post* (Pittsburg, PA) Aug. 11, 1899.
25. Unknown. "Among the Pugs". *The Pittsburg Press* (Pittsburg, PA) Aug. 23, 1899.
26. Unknown. "Among the Pugs". *The Pittsburg Press* (Pittsburg, PA) Aug. 27, 1899.
27. Unknown. "Among the Boxers". *The Pittsburg Post* (Pittsburg, PA) Aug. 29, 1899.
28. Unknown. "Among the Boxers". *The Pittsburg Post* (Pittsburg, PA) Sep. 02, 1899.
29. Abrams, Al. "Sidelights on Sports". *The Pittsburgh Post-Gazette* (Pittsburgh, Pa) Sep. 18, 1952.
30. Unknown. "Fought to a Draw". *The Pittsburg Press* (Pittsburg, PA) Sep. 03, 1899.
31. Unknown. "A Fast Fight at the Pelicans". *The Sun* (New York, NY) Sep. 03, 1899.
32. Plexus, Solar. "The Boxing Game". *The Pittsburg Post* (Pittsburg, PA) Sep. 03, 1899.
33. Unknown. "Bouts at the Greenwood". *The Brooklyn Daily Eagle* (Brooklyn, NY) Sep. 04, 1899.
34. Unknown. "M'Clelland the Winner". *The Pittsburg Post* (Pittsburg, PA) Sep. 08, 1899.
35. Unknown. "All the Sporting News". *The Pittsburg Press* (Pittsburg, PA) Sep. 08, 1899.
36. Unknown. "Among the Boxers". *The Pittsburg Post* (Pittsburg, PA) Sep. 09, 1899.
37. Unknown. "M'Clelland Gets a Match". *The Pittsburg Post* (Pittsburg, PA) Sep. 20, 1899.
38. Unknown. "Among the Boxers". *The Pittsburg Post* (Pittsburg, PA) Sep. 27, 1899.
39. Unknown. "Among the Pugs". *The Pittsburg Press* (Pittsburg, PA) Sep. 30, 1899.
40. Unknown. "Pugilism in Pittsburg". *The Pittsburg Press* (Pittsburg, PA) Sep. 30, 1899.
41. Unknown. "Spectators Displeased". *The Pittsburg Press* (Pittsburg, PA) Oct. 03, 1899.
42. Plexus, Solar. "The Boxing Game". *The Pittsburg Post* (Pittsburg, PA) Oct. 09, 1899.
43. Unknown. "Among the Boxers". *The Pittsburg Post* (Pittsburg, PA) Oct. 26, 1899.
44. Unknown. "Among the Pugs". *The Pittsburg Press* (Pittsburg, PA) Nov. 15, 1899.

45. Unknown. "Fairborn Outpointed". *The Pittsburg Press* (Pittsburg, PA) Nov. 16, 1899.
46. Unknown. "Among the Pugs". *The Pittsburg Press* (Pittsburg, PA) Nov. 28, 1899.
47. Unknown. "Among the Boxers". *The Pittsburg Post* (Pittsburg, PA) Dec. 21, 1899.
48. Unknown. "Wheeling Fight Ends in a Draw". *The Pittsburg Post* (Pittsburg, PA) Dec. 22, 1899.
49. Unknown. "M'Clelland and Bolin". *The Pittsburg Post* (Pittsburg, PA) Dec. 23, 1899.
50. Unknown. "Among the Boxers". *The Pittsburg Post* (Pittsburg, PA) Dec. 24, 1899.

1900

1. Unknown. "Among the Boxers". *The Pittsburg Post* (Pittsburg, PA) Jan. 03, 1900.
2. Unknown. "Among the Boxers". *The Pittsburg Post* (Pittsburg, PA) Jan. 16, 1900.
3. Unknown. "About the Boxers". *The Pittsburg Press* (Pittsburg, PA) Jan. 27, 1900.
4. Unknown. "Among the Boxers". *The Pittsburg Post* (Pittsburg, PA) Jan. 27, 1900.
5. Unknown. "Among the Pugs". *The Pittsburg Press* (Pittsburg, PA) Feb. 05, 1900.
6. Unknown. "Among the Boxers". *The Pittsburg Post* (Pittsburg, PA) Feb. 05, 1900.
7. Unknown. "Among the Boxers". *The Pittsburg Post* (Pittsburg, PA) Feb. 11, 1900.
8. Unknown. "Among the Boxers". *The Pittsburg Post* (Pittsburg, PA) Feb. 18, 1900.
9. Unknown. "Among the Boxers". *The Pittsburg Post* (Pittsburg, PA) Feb. 22, 1900.
10. Unknown. "Ryan and M'Clelland". *The Elmira Daily Gazette* (Elmira, NY) Feb. 22, 1900.
11. Unknown. "McClelland's Decision". *Buffalo Evening News* (Buffalo, NY) Feb. 23, 1900.
12. Unknown. "Gossip of the Ring". *Buffalo Express* (Buffalo, NY) Feb. 24, 1900.
13. Unknown. "Billy Ryan says he was jobbed". *Buffalo Evening News* (Buffalo, NY) Feb. 27, 1900.
14. Unknown. "Among the Boxers". *The Pittsburg Post* (Pittsburg, PA) Mar. 08, 1900.
15. Unknown. "Fresh Jabs and Jolts". *The Pittsburg Press* (Pittsburg, PA) Mar. 15, 1900.
16. Unknown. "Successful Boxing Show". *The Pittsburg Post* (Pittsburg, PA) Mar. 15, 1900.
17. Unknown. "Among the Boxers". *The Pittsburg Post* (Pittsburg, PA) Mar. 25, 1900.
18. Unknown. "Jolts and Jabs". *The Pittsburg Press* (Pittsburg, PA) Mar. 30, 1900.
19. Unknown. "M'Clelland Won from Hamilton". *Buffalo Enquirer* (Buffalo, NY) Mar. 31, 1900.
20. Unknown. "Among the Boxers". *The Pittsburg Post* (Pittsburg, PA) Apr. 02, 1900.
21. Unknown. "Jolts and Jabs". *The Pittsburg Press* (Pittsburg, PA) Apr. 10, 1900.
22. Unknown. "Among the Boxers". *The Pittsburg Post* (Pittsburg, PA) Apr. 11, 1900.

23. Unknown. "Jolts and Jabs". *The Pittsburg Press* (Pittsburg, PA) Apr. 13, 1900.
24. Unknown. "Among the Boxers". *The Pittsburg Post* (Pittsburg, PA) Apr. 13, 1900.
25. Unknown. "Among the Boxers". *The Pittsburg Post* (Pittsburg, PA) Apr. 15, 1900.
26. Unknown. "Ryan and McClelland". *Democrat and Chronicle* (Rochester, NY) Apr. 15, 1900.
27. Unknown. "Among the Boxers". *The Pittsburg Post* (Pittsburg, PA) Apr. 19, 1900.
28. Unknown. "Ryan Won from M'Clelland". *Buffalo Enquirer* (Buffalo, NY) Apr. 27, 1900.
29. Unknown. "Among the Boxers". *The Pittsburg Post* (Pittsburg, PA) Apr. 29, 1900.
30. Unknown. "McClelland Stops Over in Buffalo". *Buffalo Enquirer* (Buffalo, NY) Apr. 28, 1900.
31. Unknown. "Jack M'Clelland Defeated". *The Pittsburg Press* (Pittsburg, PA) May. 02, 1900.
32. Unknown. "Among the Boxers". *The Pittsburg Post* (Pittsburg, PA) May. 07, 1900.
33. Unknown. "All the Sporting News". *The Pittsburg Press* (Pittsburg, PA) June. 01, 1900.
34. Unknown. "Among the Boxers". *The Pittsburg Post* (Pittsburg, PA) June. 03, 1900.
35. Unknown. "McClelland-Hamilton bout". *The Pittsburg Press* (Pittsburg, PA) June. 03, 1900.
36. Unknown. "Among the Boxers". *The Pittsburg Post* (Pittsburg, PA) June. 11, 1900.
37. Unknown. "20 Rounds to a Draw". *The Pittsburg Post* (Pittsburg, PA) June. 12, 1900.
38. Unknown. "Among the Boxers". *The Pittsburg Post* (Pittsburg, PA) June. 16, 1900.
39. Unknown. "McClelland in Good Condition". *The Pittsburg Press* (Pittsburg, PA) July. 01, 1900.
40. Unknown. "Fought to a Draw". *Pittsburg Commercial Gazette* (Pittsburg, PA) July. 03, 1900.
41. Unknown. "McClelland will try to get even". *Pittsburg Commercial Gazette* (Pittsburg, PA) July.26, 1900.
42. Plexus, Solar "The Boxing Game as told by Solar Plexus". *Pittsburg Post* (Pittsburg, PA) August. 05, 1900.
43. Plexus, Solar "M'Clelland Draws With Kid Broad". *Pittsburg Post* (Pittsburg, PA) August. 10, 1900.
44. Unknown. "Alderman Wolf Hunting Baily". *Pittsburg Post* (Pittsburg, PA) August. 13, 1900.
45. Unknown. "Both Men Are Ready". *Pittsburg Post* (Pittsburg, PA) August. 13, 1900.

46. Unknown. "Latest Doing Among Boxers". *The Pittsburg Press* (Pittsburg, PA) Sept. 03, 1900.
47. Unknown. "Knocked Moran Out". *Pittsburg Commercial Gazette* (Pittsburg, PA) Sept.04, 1900.
48. Unknown. "Pugilist on the Car". *Pittsburg Post* (Pittsburg, PA) Sept. 05, 1900.
49. Unknown. "Among the Boxers". *The Pittsburg Post* (Pittsburg, PA) Sept. 09, 1900.
50. Unknown. "Among the Boxers". *The Pittsburg Post* (Pittsburg, PA) Sept. 13, 1900.
51. Unknown. "M'Clelland Gets the Decision". *The Pittsburg Press* (Pittsburg, PA) Sept. 14, 1900.
52. Unknown. "Among the Boxers". *The Pittsburg Post* (Pittsburg, PA) Oct. 10, 1900.
53. Unknown. "M'Clelland And Henniger Are Ready To Fight". *Pittsburg Commercial Gazette* (Pittsburg, PA) Oct.11, 1900.
54. Unknown. "Decision goes to M'Clelland". *The Pittsburg Post* (Pittsburg, PA) Oct. 12, 1900.
55. Unknown. "Among the Boxers". *The Pittsburg Post* (Pittsburg, PA) Oct. 18, 1900.
56. Unknown. "M'Clelland is A Winner". *The Pittsburg Post* (Pittsburg, PA) Oct. 21, 1900.
57. Unknown. "Among the Boxers". *The Pittsburg Post* (Pittsburg, PA) Oct. 22, 1900.
58. Unknown. "Among the Boxers". *The Pittsburg Post* (Pittsburg, PA) Oct. 30, 1900.
59. Unknown. "Twenty Rounds and a Draw". *The Pittsburg Post* (Pittsburg, PA) Oct. 31, 1900.
60. Unknown. "Among the Boxers". *The Pittsburg Post* (Pittsburg, PA) Dec. 04, 1900.
61. Unknown. "Jolts and Jabs". *The Pittsburg Press* (Pittsburg, PA) Dec 15. 1900.
62. Unknown. "Among the Fighters". *The Pittsburg Press* (Pittsburg, PA) Dec. 16, 1900.
63. Unknown. "Among the Boxers". *The Pittsburg Post* (Pittsburg, PA) Dec. 17, 1900.
64. Unknown. "Twenty Rounds to a Draw". *The Pittsburg Post* (Pittsburg, PA) Dec. 19, 1900.
65. Unknown. "Among the Boxers". *The Pittsburg Post* (Pittsburg, PA) Dec. 30, 1900.

1901

1. Unknown. "Among the Boxers". *The Pittsburg Post* (Pittsburg, PA) Jan. 02, 1901.
2. Unknown. "Among the Boxers". *The Pittsburg Post* (Pittsburg, PA) Jan. 04, 1901.
3. Unknown. "Among the Boxers". *The Pittsburg Post* (Pittsburg, PA) Jan. 23, 1901.
4. Unknown. "Among the Boxers". *The Pittsburg Post* (Pittsburg, PA) Jan. 27, 1901.
5. Unknown. "McCourt Out of the Race". *The Pittsburg Post* (Pittsburg, PA) Jan. 27, 1901.
6. Unknown. "Santry Put Out By M'Clelland". *The Pittsburg Post* (Pittsburg, PA) Jan. 30, 1901.
7. Plexus, Solar. "Boxing Game by Solar Plexus". *The Pittsburg Post* (Pittsburg, PA) Feb. 04, 1901.
8. Unknown. "Among the Boxers". *The Pittsburg Post* (Pittsburg, PA) Feb. 17, 1901.
9. Unknown. "Among the Boxers". *The Pittsburg Post* (Pittsburg, PA) Mar. 03, 1901.
10. Unknown. "Bout Held Up". *Pittsburg Commercial Gazette* (Pittsburg, PA) Mar. 09, 1901.
11. Unknown. "Boxing Bouts in Coliseum". *The Morning Star* (Muncie, IN) Mar. 11, 1901.
12. Unknown. "Ready for the Opening". *The Elwood Daily* Record (Elwood, IN) Mar. 14, 1901.
13. Unknown. "Elwood's Boxing Carnival". *The Indianapolis News* (Indianapolis, IN) Mar. 18, 1901.
14. Unknown. "Ready for the Opening". *The Elwood Daily* Record (Elwood, IN) Mar. 18, 1901.
15. Unknown. "M'Clelland Knocks Out Olson". *Chicago Tribune* (Chicago, IL) Apr. 06, 1901.
16. Plexus, Solar. "Boxing Game by Solar Plexus". *The Pittsburg Post* (Pittsburg, PA) Apr. 07, 1901.
17. Siler, George. "Gilmore Discusses Ole Olson's Defeat-Tommy West goes East". *Chicago Tribune* (Chicago, IL) Apr. 08, 1901.
18. Unknown. "Fought His Way to the Front" *Pittsburg Commercial Gazette* (Pittsburg, PA) Apr. 09, 1901.
19. Unknown. "Derby Night Fights" *Pittsburg Commercial* Gazette (Pittsburg, PA) Apr. 17, 1901.
20. Unknown. "Among the Boxers". *The Pittsburg Post* (Pittsburg, PA) Apr. 21, 1901.
21. Unknown. "Among the Boxers". *The Pittsburg Post* (Pittsburg, PA) Apr. 29, 1901.
22. Unknown. "Jack M'Clelland Loses". *The Pittsburg Post* (Pittsburg, PA) Apr. 29, 1901.

23. Unknown. "Among the Boxers". *The Pittsburg Post* (Pittsburg, PA) May. 07, 1901.
24. Unknown. "Not Jack McClelland". *The Pittsburg Press* (Pittsburg, PA) June. 01, 1901.
25. Unknown. "M'Govern and M'Clelland". *The Pittsburg Press* (Pittsburg, PA) June. 01, 1901.
26. Unknown. "McClelland-Callahan Match Off". *The Pittsburg Post* (Pittsburg, PA) July. 29, 1901.
27. Unknown. "Kennedy Matched". *The Pittsburg Press* (Pittsburg, PA) Aug. 04, 1901.
28. Unknown. "Among the Boxers". *The Pittsburg Post* (Pittsburg, PA) Aug. 11, 1901.
29. Unknown. "Benefit for the Strikers". *The Pittsburg Press* (Pittsburg, PA) Aug. 11, 1901.
30. Unknown. "M'Clelland at Kittanning". *The Pittsburg Post* (Pittsburg, PA) Aug. 11, 1901.
31. Unknown. "Among the Boxers". *The Pittsburg Post* (Pittsburg, PA) Aug. 21, 1901.
32. Unknown. "M'Clelland Gets The Decision". *The Pittsburg Post* (Pittsburg, PA) Aug. 22, 1901.
33. Unknown. "Eddie Kennedy in Training". *The Pittsburg Press* (Pittsburg, PA) Sept. 22, 1901.
34. Unknown. "Match for M'Clelland". *The Pittsburg Press* (Pittsburg, PA) Oct. 06, 1901.
35. Unknown. "Among the Boxers". *The Pittsburg Post* (Pittsburg, PA) Oct. 10, 1901.
36. Unknown. "Fresh from the Ring". *The Pittsburg Press* (Pittsburg, PA) Nov. 13, 1901.
37. Unknown. "About the Fighters". *The Pittsburg Press* (Pittsburg, PA) Nov. 17, 1901.
38. Unknown. *"McClelland Will Meet Callahan". The Pittsburg Post* (Pittsburg, PA) Nov. 17, 1901.
39. Unknown. *"Hamilton Arrives in New Castle". The Pittsburg Post* (Pittsburg, PA) Nov. 20, 1901.
40. Unknown. *"Contest Ended in Draw". The Pittsburg Post* (Pittsburg, PA) Nov. 22, 1901.
41. Unknown. *"Among the Boxers". The Pittsburg Post* (Pittsburg, PA) Nov. 23, 1901.

1902

1. Unknown. "M'Clelland Out Again". *The Pittsburg Press* (Pittsburg, PA) Jan. 19, 1902.
2. Unknown. "M'Clelland Coming Aboard". *The Pittsburg Press* (Pittsburg, PA) Feb. 02, 1902.
3. Unknown. "M'Clelland Fights on Wednesday". *The Pittsburg Press* (Pittsburg, PA) Feb. 16, 1902.
4. Unknown. "M'Clelland and Santry". *The Inter Ocean* (Chicago, IL) Feb. 19, 1902.
5. Unknown. "Eddie Santry A Lucky Boy". *The Pittsburg Post* (Pittsburg, PA) Feb. 20, 1902.
6. Unknown. "Santry Lucky to Get a Draw". Chicago Tribune (Chicago, IL) Feb. 20, 1902.
7. Unknown. "Among the Boxers". *The Pittsburg Post* (Pittsburg, PA) Mar. 01, 1902.
8. Unknown. "Among the Boxers". *The Pittsburg Post* (Pittsburg, PA) Mar. 05, 1902.
9. Unknown. "Ryan to Box M'Clelland". *The Inter Ocean* (Chicago, IL) Mar. 06, 1902.
10. Unknown. "M'Clelland Gets a Draw". *The Pittsburg Post* (Pittsburg, PA) Mar. 07, 1902.
11. Unknown. "Ryan and M'Clelland Draw". *Chicago Tribune* (Chicago, IL) Mar. 07, 1902.
12. Unknown. "To Train at Denver". *The Pittsburg Press* (Pittsburg, PA) Mar. 16, 1902.
13. Unknown. "Jack M'Clelland in Denver". *The Pittsburg Post* (Pittsburg, PA) Mar. 24, 1902.
14. Unknown. "Police to Stop the Fight". *The Pittsburg Post* (Pittsburg, PA) Mar. 27, 1902.
15. Unknown. "Bars Professional Element". *Chicago Tribune* (Chicago, IL) Mar. 28, 1902.
16. Unknown. "Young Corbett Hunting Snaps". *The Pittsburg Press* (Pittsburg, PA) Apr. 06, 1902.
17. Unknown. "Fight Stopped in the Third". *The Pittsburg Post* (Pittsburg, PA) Apr. 20, 1902.
18. Unknown. "M'Clelland at Work". *The Pittsburg Press* (Pittsburg, PA) May. 25, 1902.
19. Unknown. "Hard Work for M'Clelland". *The Pittsburg Press* (Pittsburg, PA) May. 28, 1902.
20. Unknown. "Six Round No Decision". *The Pittsburg Post* (Pittsburg, PA) June. 03, 1902.
21. Unknown. "Exhibition Not a Contest". *The Pittsburg Press* (Pittsburg, PA) June. 03, 1902.
22. Unknown. "Hot Times at Democratic Conventions". *The Pittsburg Gazette* (Pittsburg, PA) July. 02, 1902.

23. Unknown. "Wayne Will Meet Davis To-Morrow". *The Pittsburg Post* (Pittsburg, PA) Aug. 17, 1902.
24. Unknown. "Opening Show A Frost". *The Pittsburg Press* (Pittsburg, PA) Sept. 26, 1902.
25. Unknown. "Mason to Handle M'Clelland, the Boxer". *The Pittsburg Press* (Pittsburg, PA) Nov. 02, 1902.
26. Unknown. "Among the Boxers". *The Pittsburg Post* (Pittsburg, PA) Nov. 14, 1902.
27. Unknown. "M'Clelland Fights To-night". *The Pittsburg Post* (Pittsburg, PA) Nov. 20, 1902.
28. Unknown. "Sullivan and Trainer Whipped By M'Clelland". *The Pittsburg Press* (Pittsburg, PA) Nov. 21, 1902.
29. Unknown. "M'Clelland the Winner". *The Pittsburg Post* (Pittsburg, PA) Nov. 21, 1902.
30. Unknown. "M'Clelland Is Tipped To Win From Dave Sullivan." *The Pittsburg Press* (Pittsburg, PA) Nov. 24, 1902.
31. Unknown. "May Give Too Much Weight". *The Pittsburg Post* (Pittsburg, PA) Nov. 21, 1902.
32. Unknown. "M'Clelland Match". *The Pittsburg Gazette* (Pittsburg, PA) Nov. 25, 1902.
33. Unknown. "M'Clelland Robbed By Saint Louis Referee". *The Pittsburg Press* (Pittsburg, PA) Nov. 28, 1902.
34. Unknown. "M'Clelland Loses Fight To Eddie Toy". *The Pittsburg Post* (Pittsburg, PA) Nov. 28, 1902.
35. Unknown. "Ed Toy Won On Points Says St. Louis Special". The Pittsburg *Press (Pittsburg, PA) Nov. 29, 1902.*
36. *Unknown.* "Referee Defended". The Pittsburg Press (Pittsburg, PA) Nov. 30, 1902.
37. Unknown. "M'Clelland Starts for Michigan Tonight". *The Pittsburg Press* (Pittsburg, PA) Dec. 07, 1902.
38. Unknown. "Referee Called the Bout a Draw". *The Pittsburg Gazette* (Pittsburg, PA) Dec. 10, 1902.
39. Unknown. *"McClelland Bout at St. Louis". The Pittsburg Post* (Pittsburg, PA) Dec. 14, 1902.
40. Unknown. *"M'Clelland and Eddie Toy". The Pittsburg Post* (Pittsburg, PA) Dec. 14, 1902.
41. Unknown. *"Among the Boxers". The Pittsburg Post* (Pittsburg, PA) Dec. 19, 1902.
42. Unknown. *"St. Louis Fight A Draw". The Pittsburg Post* (Pittsburg, PA) Dec. 19, 1902.
43. Unknown. *"M'Clelland Coming Home". The Pittsburg Press* (Pittsburg, PA) Dec. 19, 1902.
44. Unknown. *"A Draw in Ten Rounds". The Pittsburg Post* (Pittsburg, PA) Dec. 20, 1902.
45. Unknown. *"Among the Boxers". The Pittsburg Post* (Pittsburg, PA) Dec. 20, 1902.

46. Unknown. *"M'Clelland Will Rest"*. *The Pittsburg Press* (Pittsburg, PA) Dec. 21, 1902.
47. Unknown. *"Among the Boxers"*. *The Pittsburg Post* (Pittsburg, PA) Dec. 31, 1902.

1903

1. The Consolidated Illustrating Company. *Allegheny County Pennsylvania; Illustrated*. Pittsburg: Unknown, 1896.
2. Unknown. "Big Match Coming". *The Pittsburg Press* (Pittsburg, PA) Jan. 04, 1903.
3. Unknown. "Jack M'Clelland in High Demand". *The Pittsburg Gazette* (Pittsburg, PA) Jan. 11, 1903.
4. Unknown. "Crockey Boyle Starts For the Smoky City". *The Pittsburg Press* (Pittsburg, PA) Jan. 16, 1903.
5. Unknown. "Boyle Lost Decision on Points". *The Pittsburg Press* (Pittsburg, PA) Jan. 18, 1903.
6. Unknown. "Crockey Boyle's Wail". *The Pittsburg Press* (Pittsburg, PA) Jan. 25, 1903.
7. Unknown. "Young Corbett May Meet M'Clelland". *The Pittsburg Gazette* (Pittsburg, PA) Feb. 01, 1903.
8. Unknown. "Deal Framed Up To Beat Corbett". *The Pittsburg Press* (Pittsburg, PA) Feb. 04, 1903.
9. Unknown. "Three Good Bouts in Sight". *The Pittsburg Post* (Pittsburg, PA) Feb. 08, 1903.
10. Unknown. "Among the Boxers". *The Pittsburg Post* (Pittsburg, PA) Feb. 13, 1903.
11. Unknown. "Among the Boxers". *The Pittsburg Post* (Pittsburg, PA) Feb. 14, 1903.
12. Unknown. "M'Clelland's Hard Test". *The Pittsburg Gazette* (Pittsburg, PA) Feb. 15, 1903.
13. Unknown. "Boxing Bout is Postponed". *The Pittsburg Post* (Pittsburg, PA) Feb. 20, 1903.
14. Unknown. "Among the Pugs". *The Pittsburg Press* (Pittsburg, PA) Mar. 13, 1903.
15. Unknown. "Lively Week for Boxers". *The Pittsburg Post* (Pittsburg, PA) Mar. 15, 1903.
16. Unknown. "Among the Boxers". *The Pittsburg Post* (Pittsburg, PA) Mar. 18, 1903.
17. Unknown. "Among the Boxers". *The Pittsburg Post* (Pittsburg, PA) Mar. 19, 1903.
18. Unknown. "Among the Boxers". *The Pittsburg Post* (Pittsburg, PA) Mar. 20, 1903.
19. Unknown. "M'Clelland's Won In Ten Rounds". *The Pittsburg Gazette* (Pittsburg, PA) Mar. 22, 1903.
20. Unknown. "M'Clelland is the Winner of the Bout". *The Pittsburg Press* (Pittsburg, PA) Mar. 22, 1903.
21. Unknown. "Says M'Clelland Lost". *The Buffalo Enquirer* (Buffalo, NY) Mar. 23, 1903.
22. Unknown. "Ready For Gong". *The Pittsburg Gazette* (Pittsburg, PA) Mar. 24, 1903.

23. Unknown. "Bound For Canada". *The Pittsburg Gazette* (Pittsburg, PA) Mar. 28, 1903.
24. Unknown. "Among the Boxers". *The Pittsburg Post* (Pittsburg, PA) Apr. 02, 1903.
25. Unknown. "Says Decision Was a Bold Steal". *The Pittsburg Press* (Pittsburg, PA) Apr. 06, 1903.
26. Unknown. "Reddy Mason and McCloskey". *The Buffalo Enquirer* (Buffalo, NY) Apr. 08, 1903.
27. Unknown. "Billy Maynard Here for His Fight with M'Clelland". *The Pittsburg Press* (Pittsburg, PA) May. 23, 1903.
28. Unknown. "Says All Kinds Of Vice Must Go". *The Pittsburg Gazette* (Pittsburg, PA) May. 26, 1903.
29. Unknown. "McClelland-Maynard Bout Off". *The Buffalo Express* (Buffalo, NY) May. 26, 1903.
30. Unknown. "McClelland Knocks Out Meyer". *The Pittsburg Post* (Pittsburg, PA) May. 28, 1903.
31. Unknown. "Among the Boxers". *The Pittsburg Post* (Pittsburg, PA) June. 05, 1903.
32. Unknown. "Good Boxing Show". *The Pittsburg Post* (Pittsburg, PA) June. 07, 1903.
33. Unknown. "Among the Boxers". *The Pittsburg Post* (Pittsburg, PA) Aug. 05, 1903.
34. Unknown. "McClelland Training". *The Pittsburg Press* (Pittsburg, PA) Aug. 09, 1903.
35. Unknown. "Bowser World Hard". *The Pittsburg Press* (Pittsburg, PA) Aug. 20, 1903.
36. Unknown. "Among the Boxers". *The Pittsburg Post* (Pittsburg, PA) Aug. 24, 1903.
37. Unknown. "Was Stopped By Police". *The Pittsburg Post* (Pittsburg, PA) Aug. 25, 1903.
38. Unknown. "The Scrap Saved Smith". *The Pittsburg Press* (Pittsburg, PA) Aug. 26, 1903.
39. Unknown. "McClelland Beat Smith". *The Pittsburg Press* (Pittsburg, PA) Sep. 01, 1903.
40. Unknown. "McClelland Confident". *The Pittsburg Press* (Pittsburg, PA) Sep. 02, 1903.
41. Unknown. "Will Fight Somewhere". *The Pittsburg Press* (Pittsburg, PA) Sep. 09, 1903.
42. Unknown. "M'Clelland to Meet Hanlon". *The Pittsburg Press* (Pittsburg, PA) Oct. 03, 1903.
43. Unknown. "Is Bound To Get A Fight". *The Pittsburg Press* (Pittsburg, PA) Oct. 09, 1903.
44. Unknown. "Scored Knockout". *The Pittsburg Press* (Pittsburg, PA) Oct. 23, 1903.
45. Unknown. "Jimmy Mason on Fighters". *The Pittsburg Press* (Pittsburg, PA) Nov. 01, 1903.

46. Unknown. "M'Clelland Matched To Meet A Strong Man". *The Pittsburg Press* (Pittsburg, PA) Nov. 23, 1903.
47. Unknown. "M'Clelland Meets Neary". *The Pittsburg Press* (Pittsburg, PA) Nov. 29, 1903.
48. Unknown. "M'Clelland Is Training". *The Pittsburg Press* (Pittsburg, PA) Dec. 02, 1903.
49. Unknown. "Among the Boxers". *The Pittsburg Post* (Pittsburg, PA) Dec. 04, 1903.
50. Unknown. "Jack M'Clelland Home". *The Pittsburg Gazette* (Pittsburg, PA) Dec. 07, 1903.
51. Unknown. "Among the Pugs". *The Pittsburg Press* (Pittsburg, PA) Dec. 08, 1903.
52. Unknown. "Among the Boxers". *The Pittsburg Post* (Pittsburg, PA) Dec. 10, 1903.
53. Unknown. "Among the Boxers". *The Pittsburg Post* (Pittsburg, PA) Dec. 13, 1903.
54. Unknown. "Jimmy Hanlon Issues a Defi". *The Pittsburg Press* (Pittsburg, PA) Dec. 13, 1903.
55. Unknown. "A Worthy Opponent Is Munroe". *The Pittsburg Press* (Pittsburg, PA) Dec. 20, 1903.
56. Unknown. M'Clelland's Busy Week". *The Pittsburg Press* (Pittsburg, PA) Dec. 20, 1903.
57. Unknown. "Among the Boxers". *The Pittsburg Post* (Pittsburg, PA) Dec. 24, 1903.
58. Unknown. "The M'Clelland-Engle Go". *The Pittsburg Post* (Pittsburg, PA) Dec. 24, 1903.
59. Unknown. "Among the Pugs". *The Pittsburg Press* (Pittsburg, PA) Dec. 26, 1903.

1904

1. Mason, Jimmie. "Date for Fight Set". *The Pittsburg Press* (Pittsburg, PA) Jan. 03, 1904.
2. Unknown. "O'Brian as Manager". *Harrisburg Star-Independent* (Harrisburg, PA) Jan. 06, 1904.
3. Unknown. "Among the Pugs". *The Pittsburg Press* (Pittsburg, PA) Jan. 10, 1904.
4. Unknown. "Confidence in Both Men". *The Pittsburg Press* (Pittsburg, PA) Jan. 14, 1904.
5. Unknown. "Jimmy Hanlon Knocked Out". *The Pittsburg Press* (Pittsburg, PA) Jan. 15, 1904.
6. Unknown. "Will Fight Kid Herman". *The Pittsburg Press* (Pittsburg, PA) Jan. 18, 1904.
7. Mason, James "Local Boy Is Claiming the Title". *The Pittsburg Press* (Pittsburg, PA) Jan. 24, 1904.
8. Unknown. "Will Leave For Kansas City". *The Pittsburg Post* (Pittsburg, PA) Jan. 24, 1904.
9. Unknown. "Challenge For Herman". *The Pittsburg Press* (Pittsburg, PA) Jan. 29, 1904.
10. Unknown. "Herman Gets Decision". *The Pittsburg Gazette* (Pittsburg, PA) Jan. 29, 1904.
11. J. C. G. "M'Clelland Gets a Raw Deal". *The Pittsburg Post* (Pittsburg, PA) Jan. 31, 1904.
12. Unknown. "Some Lively Bouts". *The Pittsburg Gazette* (Pittsburg, PA) Feb. 11, 1904.
13. Unknown. "Eddie Hanlon in the Ring". *The Pittsburg Post* (Pittsburg, PA) Feb. 14, 1904.
14. Mason, Jimmie. "Munroe Has A Slim Chance". *The Pittsburg Press* (Pittsburg, PA) Mar. 06, 1904.
15. Unknown. "Among the Pugs". *The Pittsburg Press* (Pittsburg, PA) Mar. 16, 1904.
16. Unknown. "Ordered to Stop Fight". *The Pittsburg Press* (Pittsburg, PA) Mar. 16, 1904.
17. Unknown. "Among the Boxers". *The Pittsburg Post* (Pittsburg, PA) Mar. 18, 1904.
18. Unknown. "Big Featherweight Bout". *The Pittsburg Press* (Pittsburg, PA) Mar. 20, 1904.
19. Unknown. "Among the Boxers". *The Pittsburg Post* (Pittsburg, PA) Mar. 28, 1904.
20. Unknown. "Men Are Resting". *The Pittsburg Press* (Pittsburg, PA) Mar. 20, 1904.
21. Unknown. "M'Clelland Gets Decision". *The Pittsburg Post* (Pittsburg, PA) Mar. 29, 1904.
22. Unknown. "McClelland's Hard Battle". *The Pittsburg Press* (Pittsburg, PA) Apr. 03, 1904.

23. Unknown. "Premier Featherweights Will Battle For Title". *The Pittsburg Gazette* (Pittsburg, PA) Apr. 03, 1904.
24. Unknown. "Crowd Hissed Draw Decision". *The Pittsburg Gazette* (Pittsburg, PA) Apr. 05, 1904.
25. Unknown. "Won On Points". *The Pittsburg Press* (Pittsburg, PA) Apr. 05, 1904.
26. Unknown. "M'Clelland and Goodman". *The Pittsburg Press* (Pittsburg, PA) May. 04, 1904.
27. Unknown. "Meets Kid Goodman". *The Pittsburg Press* (Pittsburg, PA) May. 08, 1904.
28. Unknown. "M'Clelland is in Good Form for Upcoming Fight". *The Pittsburg Press* (Pittsburg, PA) May. 08, 1904.
29. Unknown. "Decision A Draw". *The Pittsburg Press* (Pittsburg, PA) May. 13, 1904.
30. Unknown. "Jimmy Mason At Home". *The Pittsburg Press* (Pittsburg, PA) May. 22, 1904.
31. Unknown. "He May Meet M'Clelland". *The Pittsburg Press* (Pittsburg, PA) May. 26, 1904.
32. Unknown. "McClelland Overworked". *The Pittsburg Press* (Pittsburg, PA) June. 01, 1904.
33. Unknown. "He May Meet M'Clelland". *St. Louis Post-Dispatch* (St. Louis, MO) June. 02, 1904.
34. *"Lineal Champion: Abe Attell."* Cyberboxingzone.com Last modified: Unknown
http://www.cyberboxingzone.com/boxing/attell.htm
35. Unknown. "Among the Boxers". *The Pittsburg Post* (Pittsburg, PA) June. 02, 1904.
36. Unknown. "M'Clelland Is Given Decision over Attell". *St. Louis Post-Dispatch* (St. Louis, MO) June. 03, 1904.
37. Unknown. "M'Clelland Receives Decision over Attell In Fifteen Rounds". *St. Louis Republic* (St. Louis, MO) June. 03, 1904.
38. *"Pittsburgh Boxing: A Pictorial History."* Facebook.com Last modified: Sept 11, 2015.
https://www.facebook.com/pittsburghboxing/photos/a.1415391898678247.1073741826.1415388778678559/1646497528901015/?type=1&theater
39. Unknown. "M'Clelland Gets Decision". *The Pittsburg Post* (Pittsburg, PA) June. 03, 1904.
40. Unknown. "McClelland Ambitious". *The Pittsburg Press* (Pittsburg, PA) June. 03, 1904.
41. Unknown. "Notes of the Ring". *St. Louis Republic* (St. Louis, MO) June. 04, 1904.
42. Keck, Harry. "Jack McClelland Pittsburgh's Forgotten Fighter". *Pittsburgh Sun-Telegraph* (Pittsburgh, PA) Feb. 17, 1948.
43. Keck, Harry. "Stars of Ring Evaded Matches with McClelland". *Pittsburgh Sun-Telegraph* (Pittsburgh, PA) Feb. 18, 1948.

44. Unknown. "McClelland Goes To The East". *St. Louis Republic* (St. Louis, MO) June. 22, 1904.
45. Unknown. "M'Clelland Has the Better of it". *The Pittsburg Post* (Pittsburg, PA) July. 05, 1904.
46. Unknown. "M'Clelland Has Shade". *The Pittsburg Gazette* (Pittsburg, PA) Aug. 13, 1904.
47. Unknown. "Among the Boxers". *The Pittsburg Post* (Pittsburg, PA) Aug. 15, 1904.
48. Unknown. "Ready for Fight in Sharon". *The Pittsburg Post* (Pittsburg, PA) Aug. 29, 1904.
49. Unknown. "Among the Boxers". *The Pittsburg Post* (Pittsburg, PA) Sep. 10, 1904.
50. Unknown. "Great Interest Taken In Coming Battle". *The Pittsburg Press* (Pittsburg, PA) Sept. 18, 1904.
51. Unknown. "Dunn was Badly Beaten". *The Pittsburg Press* (Pittsburg, PA) Sept. 21, 1904.
52. Unknown. "Weight Favors Stroup". *The Pittsburg Press* (Pittsburg, PA) Oct. 02, 1904.
53. Mason, Jimmie. "M'Clelland Is In Fine Form". *The Pittsburg Press* (Pittsburg, PA) Oct. 16, 1904.
54. Unknown. "At Monongahela". *The Pittsburg Press* (Pittsburg, PA) Oct. 17, 1904.
55. Unknown. "Local Boy Won". *The Pittsburg Press* (Pittsburg, PA) Oct. 18, 1904.
56. Unknown. "Among the Boxers". *The Pittsburg Post* (Pittsburg, PA) Oct. 20, 1904.
57. Unknown. "Yanger Backs Out". *The Pittsburg Press* (Pittsburg, PA) Oct. 26, 1904.
58. Unknown. "M'Clelland Gets Training". *The Pittsburg Press* (Pittsburg, PA) Dec. 09, 1904.
59. Unknown. "In the Squared Circle". *The Pittsburg Post* (Pittsburg, PA) Dec. 11, 1904.
60. Unknown. "Many Boxing Events Scheduled Tonight". *The Pittsburg Press* (Pittsburg, PA) Dec. 13, 1904.
61. Unknown. "On the Bowling Alleys". *The Pittsburg Post* (Pittsburg, PA) Dec. 18, 1904.
62. Unknown. "The Big Bout is Stopped". *The Pittsburg Post* (Pittsburg, PA) Dec. 24, 1904.
63. Unknown. "Police Are Firm on Boxing Bouts". *The Pittsburg Press* (Pittsburg, PA) Dec. 24, 1904.
64. Unknown. "Among the Boxers". *The Pittsburg Post* (Pittsburg, PA) Dec. 29, 1904.

1905

1. Unknown. "In the Squared Circle". *The Pittsburg Post* (Pittsburg, PA) Jan. 01, 1905.
2. Unknown. "Boxing Notes". *The Pittsburg Press* (Pittsburg, PA) Jan. 01, 1905.
3. Unknown. "Among the Boxers". *The Pittsburg Post* (Pittsburg, PA) Jan. 05, 1905.
4. Unknown. "Knox and Youral Tonight". *Altoona Mirror* (Altoona, PA) Jan. 07, 1905.
5. Unknown. "McClelland-Reeder Bout Off". *Philadelphia Inquirer* (Philadelphia, PA) Jan. 08, 1905.
6. Unknown. "No Fight for Jack McClelland". *The Pittsburg Post* (Pittsburg, PA) Jan. 08, 1905.
7. Unknown. "Reeder-McClelland Go Off". *Altoona Times* (Altoona, PA) Jan. 09, 1905.
8. Unknown. "Big Crowd There". *Altoona Tribune* (Altoona, PA) Jan. 09, 1905.
9. Unknown. "Sharp Fights at Primaries". *The Pittsburg Press* (Pittsburg, PA) Jan. 15, 1905.
10. Unknown. "Sports News". *Altoona Tribune* (Altoona, PA) Jan. 16, 1905.
11. Unknown. "Among the Boxers". *The Pittsburg Post* (Pittsburg, PA) Jan. 18, 1905.
12. Unknown. "Tonights Boxing Bouts". *Altoona Mirror* (Altoona, PA) Jan. 20, 1905.
13. Unknown. "Among the Boxers". *The Pittsburg Post* (Pittsburg, PA) Feb. 09, 1905.
14. Unknown. "McClelland and McCoy Will Meet". *The Pittsburg Gazette* (Pittsburg, PA) Mar. 09, 1905.
15. Unknown. "Among the Boxers". *The Pittsburg Post* (Pittsburg, PA) Mar. 12, 1905.
16. Unknown. "Among the Boxers". *The Pittsburg Post* (Pittsburg, PA) Mar. 15, 1905.
17. Unknown. "Boxers Chosen". *The Pittsburg Press* (Pittsburg, PA) Mar. 22, 1905.
18. Unknown. "Among the Boxers". *The Pittsburg Post* (Pittsburg, PA) Apr. 08, 1905.
19. Unknown. "McClelland Matched". *The Pittsburg Press* (Pittsburg, PA) Apr. 08, 1905.
20. Unknown. "Inside the Squared Circle". *The Pittsburg Post* (Pittsburg, PA) Apr. 09, 1905.
21. Unknown. "Among the Boxers". *The Pittsburg Post* (Pittsburg, PA) Apr. 12, 1905.
22. Unknown. "McClelland vs Martin". *The Pittsburg Press* (Pittsburg, PA) Apr. 16, 1905.

23. Unknown. "Among the Boxers". *The Pittsburg Post* (Pittsburg, PA) Apr. 16, 1905.
24. Unknown. "A Hard Six-Round Bout". *The Pittsburg Post* (Pittsburg, PA) Apr. 18, 1905.
25. Unknown. "Among the Boxers". *The Pittsburg Post* (Pittsburg, PA) Apr. 19, 1905.
26. Unknown. "All Bouts Called Draw". *The Pittsburg Gazette* (Pittsburg, PA) Apr. 21, 1905.
27. Unknown. "Phenicie Finished Welsh". *The Pittsburg Press* (Pittsburg, PA) Apr. 21, 1905.
28. Unknown. "Winner Is To Meet Young Corbett". *The Pittsburg Post* (Pittsburg, PA) Apr. 21, 1905.
29. Unknown. "Among the Boxers". *The Pittsburg Post* (Pittsburg, PA) Apr. 23, 1905.
30. Unknown. "McClelland and Broad". *The Pittsburg Press* (Pittsburg, PA) Apr. 24, 1905.
31. Unknown. "No Fight Is Pulled Off". *The Pittsburg Post* (Pittsburg, PA) Apr. 25, 1905.
32. Unknown. "Among The Pugs". *The Pittsburg Press* (Pittsburg, PA) Apr. 26, 1905.
33. Unknown. "Larry Temple in Good Form". *The Pittsburg Post* (Pittsburg, PA) June. 05, 1905.
34. Unknown. "Riot In The Ring". *The Pittsburg Press* (Pittsburg, PA) June. 06, 1905.
35. Unknown. "Fight At Monongahela". *The Pittsburg Post* (Pittsburg, PA) June. 06, 1905.
36. Unknown. "McClelland Released". *The Pittsburg Press* (Pittsburg, PA) June. 07, 1905.
37. Unknown. "Woman Complains About Husband". *The Pittsburg Press* (Pittsburg, PA) June. 12, 1905.
38. Unknown. "Judge Scores a Jury". *The Pittsburg Post* (Pittsburg, PA) June. 22, 1905.
39. Unknown. "Lectured the Jury". *The Pittsburg Press* (Pittsburg, PA) June. 22, 1905.
40. Unknown. "Jury Gets a Roast". *The Pittsburg Gazette* (Pittsburg, PA) June. 22, 1905.
41. Mason, James. "Mason's Talk on Pugilism". *The Pittsburg Press* (Pittsburg, PA) July. 30, 1905.
42. Unknown. "McClelland Finishes His Training". *The Pittsburg Post* (Pittsburg, PA) July. 31, 1905.
43. Unknown. "Fought To A Draw". *The Pittsburg Press* (Pittsburg, PA) Aug. 01, 1905.
44. Unknown. "Sporting". *The Pittsburg Post* (Pittsburg, PA) Aug. 12, 1905.
45. Unknown. "Boxing Notes". *The Pittsburg Press* (Pittsburg, PA) Aug. 13, 1905.

46. Mason, Jimmie. "Mason Talks Fighters". *The Pittsburg Press* (Pittsburg, PA) Aug. 13, 1905.
47. Unknown. "Mason Is Arrested". *The Pittsburg Post* (Pittsburg, PA) Sep. 29. 1905.
48. Mason, Jimmie. "A Local Critic on Boxing". *The Pittsburg Press* (Pittsburg, PA) Oct. 01, 1905.
49. Unknown. "Mason Files Answer". *The Pittsburg Post* (Pittsburg, PA) Oct. 08. 1905.
50. Unknown. "Hanlon Bests a Heavyweight". *The Pittsburg Press* (Pittsburg, PA) Nov. 18, 1905.
51. Unknown. "Sluggest Was Gallant". *The Pittsburg Press* (Pittsburg, PA) Dec. 12, 1905.
52. Unknown. "With Padded Mits". *The Pittsburg Press* (Pittsburg, PA) Dec. 13, 1905.
53. Unknown. "Fines a Prize Fighter for Beating up a Negro". *The Pittsburg Gazette* (Pittsburg, PA) Dec. 13, 1905.
54. Unknown. "In the Roped Arena". *The Pittsburg Press* (Pittsburg, PA) Dec. 16, 1905.

1906-1909

1. Unknown. "Carter against M'Clelland". *The Pittsburg Gazette* (Pittsburg, PA) Jan. 04, 1906.
2. Unknown. "No Title Given". *The Pittsburg Press* (Pittsburg, PA) Feb. 25, 1906.
3. Unknown. "Policeman Are First At Table". *The Pittsburg Gazette* (Pittsburg, PA) Apr. 16, 1906.
4. Unknown. "Raids Are Continued". *The Pittsburg Press* (Pittsburg, PA) Apr. 16, 1906.
5. Unknown. "Lively Shooting Affair". *The Pittsburg Press* (Pittsburg, PA) Aug. 06, 1906.
6. Unknown. "SoHo Air Is Filled By Reign of Bullets". *The Pittsburg Gazette* (Pittsburg, PA) Aug. 06, 1906.
7. Unknown. "Hill District Has Furious Race Riot". *The Pittsburg Post* (Pittsburg, PA) Aug. 06, 1906.
8. Unknown. "Rioters Must Answer In Court". *The Pittsburg Post* (Pittsburg, PA) Aug. 06, 1906.
9. Unknown. "Notes from the Court". *The Pittsburg Post* (Pittsburg, PA) Aug. 17, 1906.
10. Unknown. "M'Clelland Gives Bail". *The Pittsburg Press* (Pittsburg, PA) Aug. 06, 1906.
11. Unknown. "Must Issue a Capias". *The Pittsburg Press* (Pittsburg, PA) Oct. 14, 1906.
12. Unknown. "Among the Boxers". *The Pittsburg Post* (Pittsburg, PA) Oct. 30, 1906.
13. Unknown. "Among the Boxers". *The Pittsburg Gazette-Times* (Pittsburg, PA) Nov. 28, 1906.
14. Unknown. "Among the Boxers". *The Pittsburg Gazette-Times* (Pittsburg, PA) Jan. 11, 1907.
15. Unknown. "Among the Boxers". *The Pittsburg Post* (Pittsburg, PA) Feb. 12, 1907.
16. Unknown. "Greensburg Bout Fast". *The Pittsburg Post* (Pittsburg, PA) Feb. 14, 1907.
17. Unknown. "Among the Boxers". *The Pittsburg Gazette-Times* (Pittsburg, PA) Feb. 15, 1907.
18. Unknown. "M'Clelland's On Trial". *The Pittsburg Press* (Pittsburg, PA) Feb. 18, 1907.
19. Unknown. "Notes from the Court". *The Pittsburg Post* (Pittsburg, PA) Feb. 20, 1907.
20. Unknown. "M'Clelland's Convicted". *The Pittsburg Press* (Pittsburg, PA) Feb. 20, 1907.
21. Unknown. "To Call Directors of Organizations". *The Pittsburg Post* (Pittsburg, PA) Mar. 02, 1907.
22. Mason, Jimmie. "Jimmy Mason Picks Abe Attell To Defeat Clever Englishmen". *The Pittsburg Press* (Pittsburg, PA) Dec. 29, 1907.

23. Unknown. "Among the Boxers". *The Pittsburg Post* (Pittsburg, PA) Feb. 02, 1908.
24. Unknown. "Among the Boxers". *The Pittsburg Post* (Pittsburg, PA) Feb. 04, 1908.
25. Unknown. "Among the Boxers". *The Pittsburg Post* (Pittsburg, PA) Feb. 06, 1908.
26. Unknown. "Among the Boxers". *The Pittsburg Post* (Pittsburg, PA) Feb. 06, 1908.
27. Unknown. "M'Clelland and Tyler to Fight in Ambridge". *The Pittsburg Press* (Pittsburg, PA) Feb. 06, 1908.
28. Unknown. "Six Good Boxing Bouts Held In Lawrenceville". *The Pittsburg Post* (Pittsburg, PA) Feb. 07, 1908.
29. Unknown. "Boxers Ready For the Fight". *The Pittsburg Press* (Pittsburg, PA) Feb. 09, 1908.
30. Mason, Jimmie. "Battler Sidestepping A Return Match With Boar". *The Pittsburg Press* (Pittsburg, PA) Feb. 09, 1908.
31. Unknown. "Among the Boxers". *The Pittsburg Post* (Pittsburg, PA) Feb. 10, 1908.
32. Mason, Jimmie. "Kid Tyler Is Determined to Win". *The Pittsburg Press* (Pittsburg, PA) Feb. 12, 1908.
33. Unknown. "Tyler Outpointed McClelland but Fight Is Declared a Draw". *The Pittsburg Post* (Pittsburg, PA) Feb. 10, 1908.
34. Unknown. "A Draw in Ambridge". *The Pittsburg Gazette-Times* (Pittsburg, PA) Feb. 13, 1908.
35. Unknown. "Phenicie May Meet Coulon". *The Pittsburg Press* (Pittsburg, PA) Feb. 16, 1908.
36. Mason, Jimmie. "Hats off To Tommie Burns, Says Jim Mason". *The Pittsburg Press* (Pittsburg, PA) Feb. 12, 1908.
37. Unknown. "Among the Boxers". *The Pittsburg Gazette-Times* (Pittsburg, PA) Feb. 20, 1908.
38. Unknown. "Find Starving Family". *The Pittsburg Gazette-Times* (Pittsburg, PA) Mar. 21, 1908.
39. *Cahal, Sherman "Mayview State Hospital."* Abandononline Last modified: 2016. http://abandonedonline.net/locations/hospitals/mayview-state-hospital/
40. Unknown. "Among the Boxers". *The Pittsburg Post* (Pittsburg, PA) Mar. 26, 1908.
41. Unknown. "Among the Boxers". *The Pittsburg Post* (Pittsburg, PA) Apr. 03, 1908.
42. Unknown. "Among the Boxers". *The Pittsburg Post* (Pittsburg, PA) Apr. 07, 1908.
43. Unknown. "Tame Fight in Monessen". *The Pittsburg Post* (Pittsburg, PA) Apr. 14, 1908.
44. Unknown. "Prizefighter Faces Court". *The Pittsburg Post* (Pittsburg, PA) Aug. 01, 1908.
45. Unknown. "Pugilist Sent to Jail: Didn't Support Family". *The Pittsburg Press* (Pittsburg, PA) Oct. 10, 1908.

46. Unknown. "Pugilist Sent to Jail". *The Pittsburg Post* (Pittsburg, PA) Oct. 11, 1908.
47. Unknown. "Unusual Cases in Upper Court Session". *The Pittsburg Post* (Pittsburg, PA) Oct. 11, 1908.
48. Unknown. "Jack M'Clelland Leaves the Jail". *The Pittsburg Press* (Pittsburg, PA) Jan. 16, 1909.
49. Unknown. "Jack McClelland is Freed". *The Pittsburg Post* (Pittsburg, PA) Jan. 17, 1909.
50. Unknown. "Kubiak And Tony Ross To Meet Here Tuesday". *The Pittsburg Press* (Pittsburg, PA) Jan. 24, 1909.
51. Unknown. "Among the Boxers". *The Pittsburg Post* (Pittsburg, PA) Jan. 26, 1909.
52. Unknown. "Among the Boxers". *The Gazette-Times* (Pittsburg, PA) Jan. 30, 1909.
53. Unknown. "Brannigan Draws With Fitzgerald in Spectacular Six-Round Bout". *The Pittsburg Post* (Pittsburg, PA) Jan. 26, 1909.
54. Unknown. "Among the Boxers". *The Pittsburg Post* (Pittsburg, PA) Feb. 05, 1909.
55. Unknown. "Among the Boxers". *The Pittsburg Post* (Pittsburg, PA) Feb. 10, 1909.
56. Unknown. "Jack M'Clelland Will Stage Some Good Bouts". *The Pittsburg Press* (Pittsburg, PA) Feb. 11, 1909.
57. Unknown. "Manning Knocked Out". *The Gazette-Times* (Pittsburg, PA) Feb. 13, 1909.
58. Unknown. "Berger Knocks Manning Out During Second Round of Fast Bout". *The Pittsburg Post* (Pittsburg, PA) Feb. 13, 1909.
59. Unknown. "Kennedy and More Are Ready For Their Bout". *The Pittsburg Press* (Pittsburg, PA) Mar. 11, 1909.
60. Unknown. "Lynch To Meet Moore". *The Gazette-Times* (Pittsburg, PA) Apr. 12, 1909.
61. Unknown. "Fight Is Called Off". *The Pittsburg Post* (Pittsburg, PA) Apr. 13, 1909.
62. Unknown. "Bouts Tonight At the Sterling Club". *The Pittsburg Press* (Pittsburg, PA) Apr. 17, 1909.

1910-1911

1. Jab, Jim. "Fistic Foibles". *The Pittsburg Press* (Pittsburg, PA), Aug. 05, 1910.
2. Unknown. "Among the Boxers". *The Pittsburg Post* (Pittsburg, PA) Aug. 25, 1910.
3. Unknown. "McClelland to Fight". *The Pittsburg Press* (Pittsburg, PA), Sep. 16, 1910.
4. Unknown. "McClelland to Try Again". *The Pittsburg Press* (Pittsburg, PA), Sep. 18, 1910.
5. Unknown. "Jack M'Clelland Beat Wilkinsburg Boxer". *The Pittsburg Post* (Pittsburg, PA) Sep. 24, 1910.
6. Unknown. "M'Clelland Comes Back and Wins". *The Gazette-Times* (Pittsburg, PA) Sep. 24, 1910.
7. Unknown. "Ring Notes". *The Pittsburg Post* (Pittsburg, PA) Oct. 03, 1910.
8. Unknown. "Northern Club to Resume Saturday". *The Pittsburg Press* (Pittsburg, PA), Oct. 05, 1910.
9. Unknown. "Bantams in Fast Draw". *The Pittsburg Post* (Pittsburg, PA) Oct. 09, 1910.
10. Unknown. "M'Clelland Is Beaten". *The Gazette-Times* (Pittsburg, PA) Oct. 09, 1910.
11. Jab, Jim. "Fistic Foibles". *The Pittsburg Press* (Pittsburg, PA), Oct. 11, 1910.
12. Unknown. "Battling Terry after Knockout". *The Pittsburg Press* (Pittsburg, PA), Oct. 13, 1910.
13. Unknown. "Boxing Bouts for Tonight". *The Pittsburg Post* (Pittsburg, PA) Oct. 15, 1910.
14. Unknown. "Trendell Defeats Game Battling Terry". *The Gazette-Times* (Pittsburg, PA) Oct. 15, 1910.
15. Jab, Jim. "Trendell Best Battling Terry". *The Pittsburg Press* (Pittsburg, PA), Oct. 15, 1910.
16. Unknown. "Morgan and Tom M'Mahon to Battle This Evening". *The Pittsburg Press* (Pittsburg, PA), Nov. 05, 1910.
17. Unknown. "M'Clelland Has the Punch". *The Gazette-Times* (Pittsburg, PA) Nov. 06, 1910.
18. Jab, Jim. "Knockout Scored By Tommy M'Mahon". *The Pittsburg Press* (Pittsburg, PA), Nov. 06, 1910.
19. Unknown. "Among the Boxers". *The Gazette-Times* (Pittsburg, PA) Nov. 18, 1910.
20. Unknown. "Cotton and Reed Box on Saturday". *The Pittsburg Press* (Pittsburg, PA), Nov. 22, 1910.
21. Unknown. "George Cotton Resents Change Made By Rival". *The Pittsburg Press* (Pittsburg, PA), Nov. 22, 1910.
22. Jab, Jim. "Kid Cotton Won in the First Round over Jack Reed". *The Pittsburg Press* (Pittsburg, PA), Nov. 27, 1910.

23. Unknown. "Jack Reed Knocked Out By Kid Cotton". *The Gazette-Times* (Pittsburg, PA) Nov. 27, 1910.
24. Unknown. "Brannigan at Benefit". *The Pittsburg Press* (Pittsburg, PA), Dec. 12, 1910.
25. Unknown. "Dwyer Tickets Selling Fast". *The Gazette-Times* (Pittsburg, PA) Dec. 12, 1910.
26. Unknown. "Riley-M'Closkey bout Attractive". *The Pittsburg Press* (Pittsburg, PA), Dec. 15, 1910.
27. Unknown. "Local Boxers to Be Busy". *The Pittsburg Post* (Pittsburg, PA) Dec. 16, 1910.
28. Unknown. "Among the Boxers and Wrestlers". *The Gazette-Times* (Pittsburg, PA) Dec. 17, 1910.
29. Jab, Jim. "Jack M'Clelland Knocked Out by Jeddy M'Fadden". *The Pittsburg Press* (Pittsburg, PA), Dec. 18, 1910.
30. Unknown. "M'Clelland Knocked Out By M'Fadden". *The Gazette-Times* (Pittsburg, PA) Dec. 18, 1910.
31. Unknown. "Among the Boxers Here and Elsewhere". *The Gazette-Times* (Pittsburg, PA) Mar. 21, 1911.
32. Unknown. "Glover will take Loughrey's Place". *The Pittsburg Press* (Pittsburg, PA), Mar. 23, 1911.
33. Jab, Jim. "Perry and Berger Fight a Fast Draw". *The Pittsburg Press* (Pittsburg, PA), Mar. 23, 1911.
34. Unknown. "Hiland Club to Reopen". *The Pittsburg Press* (Pittsburg, PA), Apr. 13, 1911.
35. Unknown. "Jock Simco in Best Condition of Career". *The Pittsburg Press* (Pittsburg, PA), Apr. 14, 1911.
36. Unknown. "Local Boxers Busy Tonight". *The Pittsburg Post* (Pittsburg, PA) Apr. 19, 1911.
37. Unknown. "Simco the Victor". *The Gazette-Times* (Pittsburg, PA) Apr. 19, 1911.
38. Unknown. "Buck Crouse Has Best of Abbot in Six Rounds". *The Pittsburgh Post* (Pittsburgh, PA) Sep. 05, 1911.

1912-1954

1. Guy, Richard. "Jack McClelland and Klaus Pittsburgh's Best Ring Artists". *The Gazette-Times* (Pittsburgh, PA) Feb. 23, 1913.
2. Jab, Jim. "Fistic Foibles". *The Pittsburgh Press* (Pittsburgh, PA), Jan. 25, 1914.
3. Guy, Richard. "With the Boxers". *The Gazette-Times* (Pittsburgh, PA) Aug. 29, 1915.
4. Guy, Richard. "With the Boxers". *The Gazette-Times* (Pittsburgh, PA) Jan. 02, 1916.
5. Jab, Jim. "Fistic Foibles". *The Pittsburgh Press* (Pittsburgh, PA), Feb. 23, 1917.
6. Unknown. "Old Timers Will Box At M'Isaacs Benifit". *The Pittsburgh Press* (Pittsburgh, PA), Nov. 27, 1917.
7. Guy, Richard. "With the Boxers". *The Gazette-Times* (Pittsburgh, PA) Dec. 02, 1917.
8. Guy, Richard. "Old Timers To Meet At Benefit Show". *The Gazette-Times* (Pittsburgh, PA) Dec. 04, 1917.
9. Gibson, Florent. "Friendly Punches Fly at McIsaacs' Show". *Pittsburgh Post* (Pittsburgh, PA) Dec. 14, 1917.
10. Jab, Jim. "Ring Reminiscences". *The Pittsburgh Press* (Pittsburgh, PA), Jan. 28, 1918.
11. Guy, Richard. "With the Boxers". *The Gazette-Times* (Pittsburgh, PA) Sep. 01, 1918.
12. Ralston, Guy L."When Anson Was Caught Napping". *The Gazette-Times* (Pittsburgh, PA) Jan. 28, 1923.
13. Danver, Charles F."Pittsburghesque". *Pittsburgh Post-Gazette* (Pittsburgh, PA) Apr. 11, 1930.
14. Unknown. "Dr. McClelland's Father Dies". *The Pittsburgh Press* (Pittsburgh, PA), Mar. 07, 1938.
15. Unknown. "McClelland Misses Chance". *The Pittsburgh Press* (Pittsburgh, PA), Sep. 24, 1939.
16. Unknown. "Jack McClelland, Ex-Boxer Dies". *The Pittsburgh Press* (Pittsburgh, PA), Nov. 19, 1954.

www.ingramcontent.com/pod-product-compliance
Lightning Source LLC
Chambersburg PA
CBHW070354240426
43671CB00013BA/2494